Tending the Flame

Tending the Flame

The Art of
Unitarian Universalist Parenting

Michelle Richards

SKINNER HOUSE BOOKS

BOSTON

for Shannon and Carson,
my daughter and my son,
the two people who taught me the most
about parenting

Printed in the United States

Cover design by Kathryn Sky-Peck
Cover art House Caravan, © Holly Hauser
Text design by Suzanne Morgan

ISBN 1-55896-563-7
978-1-55896-563-8

6 5 4 3 2 1
12 11 10

Library of Congress Cataloging-in-Publication Data

Richards, Michelle.
  Tending the flame : the art of Unitarian Universalist parenting / Michelle Richards.
    p. cm.
  ISBN-13: 978-1-55896-563-8 (pbk. : alk. paper)
  ISBN-10: 1-55896-563-7 (pbk. : alk. paper) 1. Christian education--Home training. 2. Parenting--Religious aspects--Unitarian Universalist Association. 3. Unitarian Universalist Association--Doctrines. I. Title.
  BV4529
  248.8'45--dc22
                        2009041563

Contents

Introduction   ix

The Learning Curve
    Know Thyself   1
    Teachable Moments   11

Rituals, Traditions and Spiritual Practices
    Family Rituals   19
    Holidays   31
    Spiritual Practices   43

Our Principles
    Inherent Worth and Dignity   65
    Justice, Equity and Compassion   75
    Spiritual Growth in Our Congregations   83
    The Search for Truth and Meaning   91
    The Right of Conscience   101
    Peace, Liberty and Justice for All   107
    The Interdependent Web   121

Big Questions and Tough Stuff
    God and the Bible   133
    The Interfaith Family   143
    Death and Grief   151
    Sexuality and Love   165
    Letting Go   175

For Further Reading   181

Introduction

Opportunities to deepen our children's spiritual lives and enrich their faith surround us. Experiencing the awe of the Grand Canyon, witnessing a butterfly emerging from a cocoon, or enjoying the beauty of a sunrise all raise issues of faith and spirituality. As parents, we can use these teachable moments of everyday life for spiritual expression. We can help our children grow in faith and belief just as we help them learn their multiplication tables.

Likewise, the deep questions our children ask about life often arise when we least expect them: while driving to the grocery store, when a child loses a soccer game, or when she finds a dead bird in the street. Many times they come when we feel least prepared to answer them and when inspiring words can be the hardest to find: when a child sees a homeless person, when another child's religion presents obstacles to friendship, or when a loved one dies. In fact, the best parenting often takes place when things seem to be falling apart. Giving our children and youth a special loving and guiding presence at the very moments when they need us most is what true parenting is all about.

These moments can be growth experiences for us as well, as we struggle with our own emotions and issues presented by the challenges before us. Called to be present for our children before tending to ourselves, we are pushed to become better parents.

This book explores the unique challenges and joys of raising children as Unitarian Universalists. Our unorthodox faith offers a different parenting experience than do many other religious traditions—and not just because of our diverse theologies. Parents raising their children as Unitarian Universalists frequently face situations that other parents may never encounter.

Because of the range of possibilities in Unitarian Universalism, you may wonder how you as a parent could possibly begin to be an effective spiritual guide for your children and youth. You may feel not only that you don't know the answers—you don't even know what the questions are! Perhaps you were raised in a different faith and now face the challenge of creating new rituals and traditions for your family. Maybe you have left behind your childhood faith and now feel the tension between wanting some of the same experiences you had as a child and honoring your current theology. If you were unchurched as a child, you may long for what you missed—a family that practices religion together.

A 2003 report from the National Study of Youth and Religion (NSYR) explored the relationship between family closeness and the number of religious experiences a family has during the week. It showed that the family which prays or engages in spiritual activities together is more likely to produce children who have stronger, more positive relationships with their parents—even as they navigate the difficult waters of adolescence. If that isn't reason enough for families to explore their faith, a National Longitudinal Study of Adolescent Health concluded that teens who have stronger relationships with parents are significantly less likely to engage in risky behaviors such as drinking alcohol, experimenting with illegal drugs, engaging in violent behavior, or contemplating suicide.

The time families spend together is precious, especially in a culture where children and adults spend much of their time apart and parents are so often stressed over conflicts between work and family. Using some of our valuable family time to bond through spiritual practices and celebrate what it means to be a Unitarian Universalist can help make the most of it.

This book explores ways to communicate your values and suggests activities that can enrich your faith and your child's. First, it examines how parents can determine what is important to express about their beliefs and how to teach this to their children. In later chapters, it presents information on the moral and religious development of children, using family rituals and the seven Unitarian Universalist Principles as a guide for your family's spiritual journey.

As Unitarian Universalists and progressive thinkers, we recognize that there are many diverse configurations that can make up a family. Every attempt has been made to be inclusive of this diversity. The pronouns *he* and *she* are used interchangeably in this book because it is important to recognize that in most instances, these realities may apply to either a mother or father and that a parental unit may consist of two mothers, two fathers, a single parent, or a grandparent who is raising children.

For this project, I received input from hundreds of parents who have raised or are currently raising their children as Unitarian Universalists. Their experiences suggest myriad ways to rejoice in the blessings of parenting a Unitarian Universalist child. Their stories can serve as a guide on the parenting journey.

Some of the ideas mentioned in this book will likely be more meaningful to you than others. Rather than an instruction manual, this book presents many ideas, practices, and opportunities from which you can take what you find to be meaningful and leave the rest behind. Just as our diversity of theology forms a large spectrum of belief, so this book presents a wide range of ideas for raising children as Unitarian Universalists. For whether families choose to light a chalice and share meaningful words, engage in a regular meditation practice, pray together, or walk a labyrinth, they are choosing to give their children a special gift for the future: a faith tradition. And in doing so, parents also give something special to themselves.

One of the greatest joys of parenting is seeing life from a new perspective. When that new perspective brings increased awareness and insight, parents can grow in their own spirituality. Profound observations by children about the reality of life have a poignancy that can offer us a greater understanding of the world and our place within it. We may be the primary guides, but sometimes we are merely the travelers, our children guiding us on the journey.

Know Thyself

Although we may take our children to religious education classes to give them the richness that participation in a faith community offers, most such programs last only an hour or two. As parents, we are the primary religious educators of our children. They will learn their concepts of faith, morality, responsibility, and justice from us. This means we are continually challenged to examine our theological beliefs—for they not only influence our thinking and motivations, but communicate deep truths to our children.

Providing a Foundation

Many of us are concerned about indoctrinating our children with our personal beliefs. We encourage our children to question and think for themselves, but in reality they want to know what we think. Even though they are accustomed to living with some uncertainty, they learn early on that we are authority figures, so they naturally look to us in developing their early beliefs about the world.

William Doherty, who delivered the Sophia Lyon Fahs lecture at General Assembly in 2007, says he learned an important lesson from his seven-year-old son, who wanted to know what happens to us after we die. A former Catholic who was still fleeing dogmatism, Doherty feared imposing his personal beliefs on his child. So he gave the standard noncommittal answer: "Well, some people believe that after we die, we go to heaven forever. Other people believe that when we die, our life is over and we live on through the memories of people who have known and loved us."

Of course, like most parents who try to worm their way out of a firm answer, he was soon faced with a follow-up question: "But what do *you* believe?"

After some additional attempts to dance around a definitive statement, Doherty admitted that he believes we live on in the memories of those who loved us. His son responded with words that Doherty says he will never forget: "I'll believe what you believe for now, and when I grow up I'll make up my own mind."

Doherty's articulate seven-year-old was able to express a deep and true reality of faith development: Young children catch their beliefs from their parents. Later, as they mature, they are able to examine their beliefs and formulate their own conclusions.

Many adults don't fully understand what we believe ourselves. How, then, can we expect our preschoolers to come up with their own answers? After all, we don't tell our youngsters that some people think stealing is wrong, but others are okay with it, so they should decide for themselves whether to take their sister's favorite toy. We don't explain to our teenagers that some people feel taking street drugs is a bad idea because it can destroy their health or their lives, but others find it to be a great way to recreate, so they should decide for themselves whether to engage in drug use.

Yet when it comes to our theological beliefs, we find it hard to share our ideas with our children. Perhaps it stems from our own lack of conviction, or a basic insecurity that our beliefs are not valid in a culture that communicates (subtly or not so subtly) that religious views outside of the mainstream are unacceptable.

Sharing our personal religious and spiritual beliefs with our children is not indoctrination. It is offering the wisdom and insight that they eagerly seek from us—just as they look to us for guidance when choosing between right and wrong courses of action. If we are vague and ambiguous when our children ask us theological questions, we lose our opportunity to have a positive influence on them in this area. Eventually they'll stop asking us religious questions and look for answers elsewhere. Many of the other people they encounter in life will not be so hesitant to pass on their beliefs, opening up the possibility that the vacuum we leave in our children's lives will be filled with a belief system contrary to our own.

As children approach adolescence, they begin to seek sources of authority outside the family and are less influenced by their parents. But it is still important for your adolescent children to understand your personal convictions in the area of religious thought. Your ideas can serve as a safe, secure harbor from which they can explore other religious concepts while seeking their own answers.

Adolescents are notorious for swinging back and forth between the worlds of childhood and adulthood with blinding speed. They need parental guidance as much as ever while they struggle with pressures to succeed, to belong to a group, and to create their own identity. For example, when your son feels uncomfortable dating someone whose religious beliefs are very different from his, you can offer reassurance, through wisdom born out of your personal spiritual beliefs, that with the bad comes the good, or that the universe will provide, or that this, too, will pass. The questions of adolescents may be different from those of young children, but unambiguous responses are needed just the same.

The essence of what we want to give to our children and youth is healthy self-esteem, a sense of morality, clear ethics, and an understanding of the meaning of life. If we don't share our spiritual and theological thoughts with our children, we deprive them of the richness of our insights and ask them to come up with their own beliefs without giving them a solid foundation to build upon.

Exploring the Meaning of Faith

The first step in teaching children about your moral, ethical, and spiritual values is knowing what you hold sacred and of ultimate value. To accomplish this, it is important to explore what *faith* means.

Many of us learned as children that faith requires a suspension of rational thought. However, having faith in something does not necessarily mean letting go of what we know as factual. Instead, faith is believing in something we hope for but cannot be certain of. For instance, if you are having elective surgery, you may gather lots of information about the benefits and risks of the procedure. You may make a very rational choice about which doctor will perform the surgery and at what facility. Yet even with all this knowledge, it takes a certain amount of faith to undergo the procedure—faith that it will go smoothly, that you will not be the person who suffers from that rare complication, that the doctor is not distracted by personal problems. Faith requires trust and commitment.

Faith is more than merely a series of ideas about religious matters. It is the foundation from which our beliefs emerge. Faith can be felt at the core of our very being and gives meaning and direction to our lives. Possessing a deep sense of faith strengthens our sense of purpose. Since our very nature as human beings is to search for meaning and purpose in life, faith is an essential part of what it means to be human.

Think of the word *faith* as a verb, a process that arises out of our personal experiences and interactions with others. This process is shaped throughout our lives by the institutions we participate in, the people with whom we engage, and the important events of our lives that lead us to either affirm or question our faith. This idea of faith as a process of learning and shaping beliefs is what our children need to learn from us in order to begin their own journey of discovery. Whether we want to or not, we will teach our children about faith and beliefs. So it only makes sense to be intentional about what we pass on to them.

Putting Your Beliefs into Words

Many of us find it difficult to describe what we believe. If you came from another religious tradition or none at all, you may find it easier to state what you *don't* believe. Even if you were raised as a Unitarian Universalist, you might not feel comfortable talking about your beliefs.

If you feel uncertain about your personal theology, you may be intimidated by the idea of articulating your beliefs to your children. But doing so doesn't have to be difficult. By taking the time to honor your spiritual yearnings, wonder about the world, and reflect on the meanings that you discover, you not only enrich our own faith, but can then share it with your children.

One way to begin is to make a list of the core values that you try to live by and most want your children to learn, such as justice, respect, trust, empathy, gratitude, generosity, and compassion.

Next, think about why those values are important to you. Although many parents may hold the same values, your reasons may be different from someone else's. Since our values form the filters through which we perceive our world and since we make conclusions based upon these perceptions, understanding why these values are important can help us discover our core beliefs. You can explore ways to express your values using simple, positive belief statements, such as:

- I believe that all people are basically good even if they do bad things.

- I believe that all people should be treated fairly and justly.

- I believe that we are all here for a reason.

- I believe that a divine presence exists in all of us.

- I believe that we can all achieve a connection to the Divine if we merely seek it.

- I believe that balance exists and that some good comes from even the bad parts of life.

Continuing Your Faith Journey

You can model for your children that faith development is a life-long journey. In addition to articulating your basic beliefs, take time to explore the richness of your faith. Since we all have different learning styles, consider the ways you learn best and how you like to express yourself as you seek answers to your own faith questions. Many congregations offer religious education programs for adults, and parents in particular, such as *Building Your Own Theology* and *Being a UU Parent*. If programs like these appeal to you but aren't offered at your congregation, let someone know you are interested, or consider leading one of these programs yourself. Whatever path you choose, the important thing is to take some deliberate steps on that journey toward understanding your own beliefs.

Practicing What You Preach

The old adage "actions speak louder than words" is especially true in matters of values and beliefs. If your actions regularly contradict your words, your children are likely to internalize what they see rather than what you say.

Usually, our actions are consistent with our beliefs. If a value is important enough to teach our children, then we will already tend to live our lives consistently with that value. When we choose an action that is consistent with our value system, it feels "right." If we act in ways that contradict our deep personal beliefs, we usually feel uncomfortable about it, even if we are unable to acknowledge or even recognize the contradiction.

Often, the very realization that our children are watching us and absorbing our values can be the catalyst for doing the right thing. For example, I personally do not like spiders, especially when they are in my house or (gasp) on my person. Yet I think it's important to teach my children to respect all of earth's creatures —and I do recognize that these creatures have an important place in the interdependent web of all existence. So I have made a concerted effort to capture them when they're in the house and place them outside in the garden, even though my immediate impulse might be to do something quite different. Knowing that my actions are being observed makes me more conscious of my behavior.

Even if consistency between words and actions is not an issue, children still need to witness us practice what we preach. If generosity is an important value to you, invite your children to help you write checks to charities or come with you to volunteer at the soup kitchen. They need to see your generosity in action, not just hear your words about why you think it is important.

Admitting Your Mistakes

Despite our best intentions, living consistently with our values can be a challenge. When our words and actions send mixed signals, children can be very perceptive and call us to task. We may feel embarrassed, but this behavior is a good sign that our children have been listening and internalizing our expressed beliefs.

In particular, we sometimes fail to live up to our ideals when interacting with our children. We don't always treat them with respect and fairness, and we may become impatient or even angry with them. This is not surprising, since no one teaches us as much about our limitations and capacity for anger as our children do. Children who are overly tired, hungry, or stimulated are prone to "push our buttons" precisely because they know where those buttons are located. We were once children, too, and may have had some negative experiences that we have not resolved or even acknowledged. Our children's actions may bring up our own anxieties, fears, or rage that we didn't even know existed.

In short, there are days when we are not particularly careful about what our behavior is teaching our children. We are human, after all. We may carry some spark of the divine and the potential to accomplish great things, but we also have moments when it just doesn't work.

Children understand this, and are more than willing to forgive—particularly if we apologize for the transgression, explain how we wish it hadn't happened, and share what we will do to make it right. In fact, these imperfect parenting moments give us an opportunity to show our children that it is okay to not be perfect—that all of us, including the people they look up to, make mistakes. By admitting our own mistakes, we teach children that when they mess up, they can make things right. We help them learn that every day carries with it the possibility and the opportunity to improve ourselves.

Using these opportunities to learn about our failings can also help to deepen the lessons we can share about values. If we agree that what we said wasn't respectful, and promise to be more mindful of the way we express ourselves, then our children learn that respect really is important to us.

Nurturing Your Own Soul

In order to nurture our children's spirituality, we must first find a way to nourish our own. Parenting can be a joy and a blessing, but it can also be draining and exhausting. If we allow others to draw from our well without any way of replenishing it, the well will quickly run dry. However, when we are feeling full spiritually, we are able to give to our children without draining ourselves and remain open to receiving their gifts of love and affection.

Yet our busy lives make it difficult to find the time we need for spiritual practices that rejuvenate our souls. Between refereeing yet another squabble between siblings and making sure all the homework gets done, it can seem impossible to find time to meditate— let alone to stay calm while the squabbling and complaining and the "I can't find my math book" is going on around us.

A "Baby Blues" cartoon that hangs on my refrigerator depicts this very dilemma. In it, the mother is attempting to do yoga while two of her three young children pepper her with questions. "What are you doing, Mom?" the girl asks.

"Yoga," the mother responds, without opening her eyes or shifting her position.

"Why?" the boy asks.

"To help relieve stress."

"Does it work?" asks the girl. "Is it working now? Maybe now?

How about now? Now?"

Then the boy asks, "Why is that vein bulging in your neck?"

We will never find time to nurture ourselves unless we make it a priority and make an intentional effort. Some parents get up earlier than their children in order to have their "quiet time." This may involve meditation, yoga, physical exercise, or just enjoying a few minutes of peace and quiet before the day begins for everyone else.

If rising early feels like torture to you, some time spent in the evening after the children are asleep may be a wiser choice. Some parents find reading an uplifting book to be a great way to feed their spiritual needs. Others like keeping a journal by their bedside to jot down poems or thoughts of what was good about that particular day.

If your time is consumed from the moment of awakening until bedtime, you may need to arrange a time to leave the house so that you can rejuvenate—even if it is only once a week. Although it may seem nearly impossible to commit to even one yoga or tai chi class a week, the benefits of doing so can be immense.

Being intentional about nurturing yourself may also mean rethinking what you need to feed your soul. If you engaged in a regular meditation practice before your children were born, but just can't seem to fit it into your new life as a parent, then maybe you need to try something new—at least until your children are older and you feel comfortable resuming this practice. A quiet walk, a glimpse of a beautiful sunset, or even a moment of peaceful quiet during nap time can be a meaningful way to recharge your spiritual self. Instead of rushing to wash the dishes while the children are napping, take the opportunity to just sit and *do nothing*.

The Zen Buddhist approach to mindfulness can also be useful. Even if we never appreciate the specialness of washing dishes mindfully—without thinking about what else needs to be done and what is yet to come—truly being present with our children can be a powerful experience. Take some time to ignore all the things you "ought" to be doing and just be with your children. Sitting on the floor with your toddler, cuddling with your six-year-old as she tells you about her day at school, hanging out with your teenager—being truly mindful of who your children are and where they are in their life journey—can be awe-inspiring. Having these connections with children and youth are so important, because they really do grow up fast. Holding on to those moments with our children and truly savoring them through awareness means we can experience the joy of parenting not just in retrospect, but right now.

Teachable Moments

Sometimes it feels as if we are sharing our parental wisdom with a brick wall. If a child is not in a position to truly process what we are trying to communicate, then our knowledge meets a wall of resistance. The key is to understand not only what children need to learn, but how we can help them be receptive to this learning. When we are sensitive to children's emotions and moral development, and when we look for the teachable moments that arise every day, we are more likely to be successful in sharing our moral and spiritual values with our children.

Emotions

While parents tend to assume that their children are most like them regarding their thinking and least like them regarding their emotions, the learning theorist Jean Piaget discovered that the reverse is actually true. Adult thinking is logical and abstract, while the thought process of children is concrete and perceptive. But children do feel embarrassment, shame, guilt, and anger, just as we do. Therefore, to communicate effectively with our children, we must not only understand how they think, but also empathize with how they feel.

People who feel overwhelmed by their emotions do not act rationally and are not open to learning. Instead, they are likely to reject any new information, say mean things, and (especially in the case of children) lash out physically. When children are feeling overly tired, hungry, or angry, they are not in a thinking mode but a reacting mode, and any attempts to appeal to them logically will fall flat.

In this case, it may be prudent to address the child's emotional outburst, recognize the overwhelming feelings that the child is experiencing, and affirm her essential goodness. Then, when time has passed and the child is no longer overwhelmed with emotions, she will be much more receptive to whatever you wish to teach.

If the parent is also in a state of high emotion, this is doubly true. Not only is the child not going to be receptive to anything she is told at this time, she is more likely to focus on and remember the parent's anger than what the parent is trying to teach. Take time to let tempers cool and equilibrium be restored. Recognize that both of you are being controlled by your emotions and that this is a fact of life. Then healing can begin, and later, when calmer heads prevail, effective communication and learning can take place.

Moral Development

Children, and even most adolescents, view moral issues much differently from the way adults do. For this reason, any attempts at moral education will be ineffective and even counterproductive unless there is some attempt to meet children at or near their level of moral reasoning. Psychologist Lawrence Kohlberg found that moral development occurs in predictable stages, and that presenting concepts just beyond a child's current stage can actually stimulate development. This is because children and adolescents generally can stretch to understand reasonings that are just beyond their current stage of moral development. However, we do children a real disservice when we force them to accept certain behaviors as "bad" before they are able to understand why.

Although your children need to understand what moral behavior you expect, you must also help them see the reasoning behind the values, the actions that they might take, and the consequences that might result from those actions. Encourage them to consider not only what the right thing to do is, but why. All this must be expressed in terms appropriate for the child's stage of development.

For example, when children younger than about seven try to decide whether someone's actions were right or wrong, they do not consider the intentions behind those actions. By posing questions about what a person was trying to do, you can help them process the idea of intentions and develop a new moral understanding.

Children around seven to ten years old may take intentions into account, but in their stage of development they are primarily focused on how relationships may be affected by wrongdoing. Emphasizing how their actions can harm or help relationships will have more influence on their behavior than punishment or lectures.

With adolescents, it will be helpful to stress the importance of rules and laws that help maintain order in our society. Since their moral development emphasizes a "law and order" mentality, stressing rules and the impact that not following those rules can have in our society is more meaningful for preteens. Persons in this life stage also have a strong tendency to see the world in terms of black and white and have difficulty discerning shades of gray. Almost everything is categorized under the headings "good" or "bad." Despite the fact that they are in an in-between stage of life, from their perspective, there is no such thing as "in-between" when it comes to areas of morality, fairness, and justice. Things are either right or wrong. Likewise, the idea that something could be true and partially false at the same time also escapes many of them. It is only later and with the development of a greater maturity that a person is able to understand that there may be times when morality requires that we violate society's rules in order to achieve a greater good.

Talking While Traveling

Sometimes our children and youth willingly offer us teachable moments by asking us questions about life. We need to be prepared to offer our wisdom during these windows of opportunity, whenever they may come. Children frequently raise difficult questions while we are driving somewhere. Although parents may not consider this an ideal time, from the child's point of view it makes sense. When you're riding in the vehicle together, they have a captive audience, yet you don't have to look each other in the eye. These circumstances can make it easier to talk about awkward or potentially embarrassing subjects.

Recognizing this reality, be prepared to answer questions when you're transporting your children to and from events. While you might be tempted to postpone the conversation until a more opportune moment, it's important to address such questions as they arise, even if they are asked during rather inconvenient times and places. Since children are most receptive to learning when they themselves initiate the experience, questions always offer a great opportunity for parents to impart their values and share spiritual understandings.

Sharing Direct Experiences

Parents often feel the need to tell their children about everything, but children have a need to experience things for themselves. It is in their nature to explore and interact with objects, handling them with their fingers (and in the case of babies and toddlers, with their mouths). It is through this direct experience that they discover the characteristics of objects and the effects of their actions on them. Says Catherine Stonehouse in *Joining Children on the Spiritual Journey*, "Discoveries made through direct experiences are more transformational and exciting for children than lessons in which adults tell them what they ought to know."

This is also true when it comes to matters of the spirit and faith development. It's one thing to tell your child about the awe you feel when you watch a beautiful sunset. When your child actually witnesses that sunset with you, the experience can not only help him better understand the awe you feel, but also create a greater connection between the two of you. There is no need for words when a direct experience shared can convey much more than talking ever could.

Encouraging Creative Play

Interacting with your child in creative play can be another way to encourage spiritual development. Kohlberg believed that role-playing is the single most important social experience for stimulating moral development. Since role-play involves putting oneself in the shoes of others—thereby becoming aware of their thoughts and feelings—it can help children step out of their egocentric world and understand what it means to affect another person. When they become aware of how their behavior affects others, then they cannot help but desire to change that behavior.

An old trunk or box full of scarves, hats, and costume jewelry can offer opportunities for skits or simply playing dress-up. At consignment shops and garage sales, you can often discover fancy hats and gloves and other fun dress-up items for little cost.

Old or broken appliances and electronic gadgets that can be disassembled stimulate the imagination. They are particularly appealing to elementary-age children who want to learn how things work. After disassembly, some of the parts can also be used for 3-D art projects or creative inventions.

Rhythm instruments (either purchased or homemade) offer a form of spiritual expression that adults and children can really delve into together. Try tapping out a steady rhythm as you encourage your child to follow along, or reflect back her sounds as she experiments with creating her own music.

Since there is often a fine line between artistic expression and spiritual expression, most creative activities can spur spiritual development. Children and youth can be encouraged to write, paint, sculpt, or even dance out their deepest thoughts and spiritual feelings. For inspiration, you might play a recording of a symphony or jazz and invite them to paint what they hear and feel. Or turn on some lively music and free yourself to dance along with your children, feeling the wonderful release of expressing your feelings without self-consciousness or fear of judgment.

Telling Stories

Often when parents try to explain issues of morality or theology to children, they feel trapped into using abstract concepts that have no relevance for children. However, children can experience these same ideas through stories. Even if children take the stories literally, focusing on only one level of their overall message, the ideas expressed by stories can still resonate deeply. In fact, according to James Fowler, a professor of theology and human development, processing stories is at the very heart of what elementary-age children need to spur growth in their faith development.

Reading to children is a great way to connect with them and encourage their faith development, but too many parents rely only on books. They miss out on the experience of telling their own stories to their children, perhaps because they lack confidence in their ability to do so. However, parents who spin their own yarns enjoy the experience of expressing themselves creatively, communicating their values in a way that is personally meaningful, and passing on the value of storytelling.

You can also encourage children and youth to tell their own stories. Storytelling helps children learn to organize and express their thoughts. The rich imagery of their imaginations can shine forth, and they can share some of their precious innate spirituality with you. According to Mimi Doe, author of *10 Principles for Spiritual Parenting*, children's stories often include deep spiritual themes. In this way, "stories can become a road map to the soul."

Elementary-age children will begin to take ownership of the stories, beliefs, and rituals valued by their respective faith communities. Their identity as individuals and as members of a faith community grows as they learn to tell the stories, recite the beliefs, and participate in the rituals that make their religion unique. While stories may not provide perfect answers, they offer the opportunity to ask questions in different ways and to try out different responses.

Many parents are concerned about the perceived scariness of some fairy tales and ancient stories, as well as about the violence and suffering present in many TV programs aimed at children. However, as rabbi Nancy Fuchs says in *Our Share of Night, Our Share of Morning*, "Children crave scary stories. Children do not want stories that claim evil does not exist. They know it does. They want stories that tell them that evil is ultimately weaker than good."

Since young children have a deep, abiding need to believe there is order and purpose in the universe, the idea that good triumphs over evil is reassuring. It also helps motivate them to do good and reap the rewards of that behavior. This is important when there is so much temptation in the world to not be compassionate, loving, and forgiving. Stories where good prevails over evil may also encourage children to articulate their inner fears and overcome their strong impulses to do what they believe is wrong. When those who stand for good in the story are rewarded in some way, then children can be reassured that they will also have the strength to prevail over danger and evil.

Family Rituals

Parents often intuitively pass down their family's traditions to their children, because the power of ritual and the need for it are far stronger than most of us realize. We may wish to provide elaborate vacations and other memorable experiences, but what often sticks in the minds of children are the everyday traditions and rituals that enrich family life and make each family's experience unique. Rituals celebrating the milestones and major transitions of life are also powerful because they affirm individuals and their experiences while bonding all of the members of the family together.

The Purpose of Rituals

Rituals provide a sense of comfort and security. They can help everyone deal with crisis, change, and transitions of a larger sort. Funerals or memorial services help us to deal with our grief, graduation parties help us to honor our youth's changing status, and various ceremonies for welcoming infants are found the world over. In fact, some biogeneticists have come to believe that ritual is part of our genetic makeup. They propose that there is a part of our brain that actually compels us to use symbols and gestures to tap into the energy of the universe or connect with the divine.

Family rituals also help build a sense of identity—not just for the child, but for the family itself. Rituals can create a sense of belonging within the family, and the shared experience builds connections to one another.

Many families have ethnic rituals that help to solidify the family's ties to their ancestral past. Some families have rituals tied to sporting events or other family interests, such as music, drama, or art. And religious families have religious traditions that tie them to their wider faith community.

Religious rituals are more than just a means of teaching theology to the next generation. They can help keep the family grounded and provide a spiritual center for everyday life. Such rituals build religious identity while opening up the possibility of exploring deeper, more personal meanings. Some of the most powerful religious rituals allow us to suspend the rational mind and allow our feeling, spiritual side to experience the sacred and our connection to the universe.

However, if the most memorable rituals of childhood are tied to the family's religious or faith tradition, and those ties have been broken by changing theological beliefs, then parents may be at a loss about how to replace them. Many parents may treasure religious rituals but reject their inherent meaning. The solution may be to create new family traditions or to tweak the old ones so that their meaning fits the family's current theology and spiritual yearnings.

Developing Family Rituals

Even though it may be a special joy to carry on a ritual just as our parents or grandparents did, our lives are very different, so we may need to invent new traditions for our own families. Since each family is actually a hybrid of two (or possibly more) families that have come together to create a new one, it only makes sense to develop some unique traditions to meet the needs of this new family.

In *The New Book of Family Traditions*, author Megan Cox recommends having one solid ritual of connection each day, as well as a modest weekly ritual. She also believes it is important for families to recognize major milestones, accomplishments, and relevant holidays. This may seem like a lot, but many of us are doing some of these things already, even if we don't recognize it. Hardly any family does without rituals of some sort—be they family jokes, annual vacation visits, or holiday traditions. Other families have adopted a family movie night with a video and popcorn, or a family game night with board or card games shared together. In fact, anything we do regularly that builds family connections, honors our heritage, passes on values, or recognizes our transitions can be considered a ritual.

To be effective and memorable, rituals do not have to be complicated. Simply marking out the space and time as something apart from the ordinary, something worthy of our attention, sets the stage for family ritual. While most rituals don't have to be elaborate, they do need to be deliberate. Since one of the functions of ritual is to pass on our values, it is important to be intentional about the rituals we create. And it is also important to take into account the true nature of our families when creating those rituals.

Although it is easier to start traditions and rituals when children are young, so that they become a part of their daily life, it is still possible to develop new rituals and traditions later on, as long as you are realistic about what works for your family. For example, it might be nearly impossible to get everyone in your family together for a peaceful dinner during the week. If this is the case, then building a meaningful ritual around family dinner probably won't be successful. A better alternative might be a family breakfast to help start the day on a positive note. Some families gather for breakfast on Saturday or Sunday, when more time is available.

Mealtime

Mealtime rituals are not only a positive venue for family connection, but also a way to create a culture of appreciation. Incorporating ritual into the everyday, ordinary act of eating a meal elevates its status in the lives of the participants.

Christine Gresser, a parent from Virginia, describes her family's mealtime ritual. Every night at dinner they light a "thankful candle," then each member of the family shares one thing that he or she is grateful for. In this ritual, family members not only share a symbol that ties them to their faith (a candle or a chalice), but also lift up the value of gratitude by stating something they are thankful for.

Saying grace or a special blessing can also be a mealtime ritual. Anne Odom explains why her family engages in this ritual: "This simple blessing before we share food together is a moment of pause in our crazy evenings. It reminds us why we share a family meal and how important we are to each other. These words have come to be very powerful for us—if it's been a rather 'snippy' evening, and we're all a little aggravated, we find that reciting the words together at dinnertime brings us all back to center again and diffuses some of that unpleasantness that was hanging around."

Some parents reject the idea of saying grace because it evokes a theology they do not embrace. However, the practice of making time to reflect on the meal and offer appreciation for it does not have to be rejected because of negative associations with a word. Most religious traditions around the world, even those which are not divinity-centered, incorporate some form of recognition of the specialness of the meal and appreciation for it. According to the website Beliefnet.com, saying grace is one of the most common and universal forms of spoken prayer, the one sacrament many of us hold on to even after others have faded from use and lost their significance.

In *Parenting with Spirit*, Jane Bartlett tells us that saying grace "makes us aware that the food in front of us is a gift. . . . In its fullest sense, saying grace is a beautiful act of awareness about our connection to the forces of nature and each other."

The words you say in your mealtime ritual can reflect your family's beliefs and pass along your values to your children. Even humanist families can relate to expressing appreciation for the farmers who grew the food, the workers who processed it, the store clerks who shelved it, and the family members who purchased it, brought it home, and prepared it. Families with more theistic beliefs might want to acknowledge God, a divine presence, or the Spirit of Life. There is no set prescription for what needs to be said, no "requirement" for what is acceptable. The simple act of lighting a chalice or candle before a meal and speaking intentionally creates a moment of sacredness and a special time for your family to recognize the purpose of your being together.

Bedtime

Children (especially young ones) need bedtime rituals to help them settle down from the busy-ness of life and relax into sleep. Going to bed also involves separation, which can be difficult for youngsters, particularly those who sleep alone in their own bedroom. Rituals can help ease this separation and provide a calm, peaceful transition to nighttime.

Most parents end up adopting some sort of bedtime ritual, whether it is intentional or not. It may simply be a bath followed by pajamas, a bedtime story, and a loving kiss. When my children were toddlers, we had a ritual of saying goodnight to everything in the house, not just the people who were in it. As we walked through the rooms saying goodnight to the refrigerator, the stove, the table, and the couch, I could literally feel my youngster relaxing, growing heavier and sleepier. By the time we made it upstairs to the bedroom, my son's head was often on my shoulder.

In *The Book of New Traditions*, Meg Cox describes a bedtime ritual that involved saying goodnight to everyone her son loved, so that he fell asleep surrounded by thoughts of people who cared about him. Cox also tells the story of Allison Defferner, who performs a bedtime ritual that her own mother began: opening the front door and reaching out to "touch" the night before bedtime.

Some parents may want to encourage their children to offer bedtime prayers, but are unsure about what words to teach them. They may remember saying prayers themselves but reject the theological underpinnings of those words, or they may have been raised unchurched or by parents who didn't believe in the value of prayer. In all of these cases, there is no need to give up on the value of prayer as a spiritual practice. Simply find the words that are meaningful to you and your family. (For some resources on prayer, see "For Further Reading" at the back of this book and for more information on prayer, see the chapter "Spiritual Practices.")

For those who do not find prayer meaningful, an alternative is meditation, either guided or silent. Guided meditations, in particular, calm the body and the mind. Children's highly developed imaginative abilities allow them to readily visualize and process the sensations described in the meditation—sights, sounds, textures, smells. You might invite your child to visualize a quiet walk in the woods, imagine floating in the starry night sky, or just focus on relaxing each part of her body in turn.

Some yoga poses, or *asanas*, are designed to deepen breathing, slow the heart rate, and relax muscles. *Matsya kridasana* (flapping fish pose) is one example; another is *makarasana* (crocodile pose). Instructions for both of these relaxing yoga poses can be found on the Internet. Tai chi—a self-paced series of slow, flowing body movements —can also be used as part of the bedtime ritual. The practice of tai chi emphasizes concentration, relaxation, and the conscious circulation of vital energy throughout the body. Tai chi practitioners focus on their breathing and the flowing movements of the body to keep their attention in the present moment, which helps calm the mind. In fact, any spiritual practice that invites relaxation, reflection, or reverence can serve as a meaningful bedtime ritual.

Bedtime stories have long been important rituals for many families. While just about any story would serve this purpose, with a little intentionality, you can use this opportunity to select stories that pass on your values. You might choose a story that addresses a question your child has asked or that focuses on a theme you want to explore with your child, such as taking care of the earth, honoring diversity, or respecting the inherent worth and dignity of all people. Pay attention to not just what issue is raised in the story, but how it is resolved. For instance, an interesting story about a boy who tricks someone may not have a resolution you perceive as just, equitable, or fair.

Bedtime stories don't have to be read—they can also be *told*. Creating your own stories is sharing your very self with your child, and that is more valuable than all the quality fiction in the world. Many parents find they truly enjoy inventing their own stories. Children love hearing these made-up tales, especially if they are featured in some grand role—perhaps a great warrior who conquers the dragon (or flies home on its back after befriending it). Older children may then be inspired to spin their own tales of adventure or mystery, sharing their thoughts and concerns, aspirations and hopes with you as they learn the value of creative self-expression.

For adolescents, bedtime rituals can provide a time of reconnection with parents after a long day of separation. A ritual established during childhood can slowly transform into a mutual sharing between parent and child as the day ends. Many parents take time to intentionally say goodnight to their teenagers (and even though the teenagers may protest and grumble, they will also be the first ones to remind their parents about it should it be forgotten). This goodnight may take the form of a simple verbal acknowledgment, a hug, or perhaps a brief time for "check-in" to share what happened during the day. Some parents use this time as a version of "joys and concerns," or simply concentrate on the "joys" part by sharing what each of them is grateful for.

The specific bedtime ritual you choose is less important than the act of doing it. So if you feel intimidated or overwhelmed by the prospect of creating meaningful, elaborate bedtime rituals, just keep it simple and from the heart.

Mornings

Parents are often advised to do everything they can to make weekday mornings go more smoothly. They are rarely encouraged to pause and reflect on the possibilities each day brings. But spending even just one or two minutes on a family ritual can help nurture spirituality and begin the day on a positive note.

Prayer is an obvious choice for some people, as is meditation, journaling, or yoga poses that promote wakefulness. Some families recite a series of affirmations, such as "Today will be a good day," or "I feel confident about today," or even "I'm alive today." Such affirmations help them focus on the moment and recognize the start of a new day with new opportunities for connections and experiences that enrich the soul.

Meg Cox, in *The New Book of Family Traditions*, suggests pausing for a connection ritual just before everyone rushes out the door. It might be a complicated handshake, a group hug, or taking turns offering "daily wishes," such as "I hope your drive to work goes smoothly" or "I hope you do well on your test today." Cox stresses that the act of tailoring the wishes to the particular day reveals that we are paying attention to each others' lives and affirms the family's connection to one another.

Weekly Rituals

For busy families that spend most of their weekdays apart, setting aside a special "family time" each week is valuable. By incorporating ritual into them, we can lift these weekly gatherings out of the ordinary and into the extraordinary.

Rabbi Nancy Fuchs says in *Our Share of Night, Our Share of Morning* that holding sacred family time once a week can be a way of taking time to *be* rather than to *do*. It is a way of asserting control by letting go. "We can say no to the phone, to technology, to work, to anything. This is the great gift of the Sabbath."

A weekly ritual might take the form of a family meeting, complete with check-ins and sharing thoughts with one another. Or you could share sacred family time over a meal—saying grace, sharing important events of the past week, singing or playing music if desired, and sharing wishes for the upcoming week. You might light a chalice or candle and say meaningful words to signify that the special family time has begun. Lighting a chalice or special candle also ties this ritual to the child's religious experiences at a

Unitarian Universalist congregation. This connection is especially important for elementary-age children, who need to understand the rituals that make their faith tradition unique.

If your family is more the outdoors type, a family walk, picnic, outing to a park, or other special time in nature may be more to your liking. Some families set aside a time each week (usually on the weekends) to engage in a social action project together. Many Unitarian Universalist congregations offer weekly or monthly "family nights," complete with a meal, a brief child-friendly worship service, and an activity for all ages.

Female Coming of Age Ceremonies

Rituals honoring a woman's first menstruation (menarche) are among the most ancient in human history and are found in cultures all over the world. Many of today's mothers, having come to appreciate the sacred aspect of a woman's changing body, want to honor their daughters' transition in ways they never experienced themselves. Many of these rituals have been impromptu and personalized to the interests and wishes of the mother and daughter. However, since more and more families are choosing to honor their daughters in this fashion, there are now numerous books, CDs, and websites that offer resources on creating a rite of passage to celebrate a young girl starting to menstruate. The ceremonies may be referred to as menarche rituals, coming of age ceremonies, first moon ceremonies, or red parties. While there may not be a set liturgy or pattern, the use of the color red is common, as is stepping over some sort of threshold or barrier. Usually a community of important women in the life of the young female is assembled to help her observe this passage.

In *Women-Church*, Rosemary Radford Ruether describes one form of menarche ceremony. At a certain point in the ritual, a baby or baby doll is given to the young woman while these words are spoken by an adult female, possibly the young woman's mother:

You are now able to become a mother. But you are not yet
ready to take responsibility for caring for another human
life, a life that will be weak and dependent on you to feed
it, wash it, clothe it and teach it how to walk and talk and
grow. You must be in control of this wonderful life-making
power of your body: do not use it until you are ready to
take responsibility for caring for another life; choose to use
it when you decide you are ready to become a mother. You
are the decision maker.

In this and perhaps all instances, parents should stress that motherhood is a choice. Even today, young girls are often taught that
motherhood is a necessary and inevitable part of growing up and
becoming a woman. This makes the pain of infertility much more
intense for those women who are unable to conceive, and it casts
suspicion on those women who choose not to become mothers.
Instead, we can teach our daughters that understanding how to care
for a baby is an important life skill, like sewing, cooking, balancing
a checkbook, and changing the tire of a car—but it is not an inevitable part of their future.

Male Coming of Age Ceremonies

Ceremonies to honor a boy's journey into manhood were also
celebrated by ancient cultures all over the world. However, until
recently, rite of passage experiences for adolescent boys have been
noticeably absent from our society. Although many boys, as well as
girls, will go through a coming of age ceremony at their Unitarian
Universalist congregation, there is seldom a special ritual for boys
corresponding to the menarche celebrations for girls. Perhaps this
is in part due to the lack of a single, significant event that clearly
announces a boy has reached puberty, as menstruation does for
females. However, the importance of a young man coming to
understand and accept the power of his own sexuality cannot be
underestimated.

Young men are hungry for such a celebration of their entry into manhood and the affirmation that rituals bring. Similar to menarche rituals for girls, celebrations for boys could bring together a community of male elders, including fathers, grandfathers, and other men who are important in their lives.

According to William Roberts Jr. in *Initiation to Adulthood*, effective coming of age ceremonies generally include three distinct stages: a rite of separation, a journey to understanding, and a rite of incorporation. The rite of separation offers powerful lessons about how the ties of mother and child are now altered. During the journey to understanding, the young males are expected to gain knowledge of themselves, their sexuality, and their spirituality. Finally, as part of the rite of incorporation, the community of men honors the individuals who are making the passage from boyhood to manhood and bestows on them new privileges and responsibilities.

Divorce

Marriage and commitment ceremonies remain among the most frequently performed rituals to mark a major transition in life. However, despite the fact that half of all marriages end in divorce, and that the impact of divorce on family members—particularly children and youth—is enormous, few rituals are performed to acknowledge the dissolution of a family. Divorce is a loss much like a death, so it makes sense to recognize that loss, just as we recognize loss of life through memorial services and funerals. Rituals for divorce can provide a sense of closure, as the couple and their children recognize the transformation of the family and begin the process of letting go.

Such a ritual would ideally have both parties present, along with the children. It would acknowledge the end of the relationship that was entered into when the couple pledged their commitment to one another. Because divorce encompasses both sorrow for the ending relationship and the promise of a new life, the ritual might include symbols of bitterness and sweetness, such as two different wines or bitter horseradish and sweet honey. Rings could be returned to one another, symbolizing the end of the bond that began when the rings were exchanged.

A new commitment or covenant could be made between the two who are parting ways, particularly if they have children. For example, this new covenant might spell out that although their relationship with one another has ended, they will remain active as parents, will support their children through this difficult transition, and will reach agreements that are in the best interest of the children.

A divorce ritual can help children understand the changing nature of their parents' relationship and begin to accept the changes that are taking place in their own lives. Without such a ritual, divorce can seem like an odd and almost unreal time for children, who may not fully understand what is happening and the significance of the changes.

First Day of School

Each year, parent Christine Sizer conducts a ritual for her children to mark the passing of another summer and the start of a new school year. This ritual brings more meaning to the transition than the traditional shopping trip to obtain school supplies. On the night before the first day of school, Christine's family lights a homemade chalice and says a prayer. Then she gives her children copies of the prayer (folded into tiny squares and taped closed) to carry in their pockets as they head off to school. Each child also chooses a palm stone from the family's beach rock collection to carry throughout the day. Finally, family members eat a celebratory dinner together.

Holidays

Holiday traditions provide continuity from year to year, and allow everyone in the family to anticipate their arrival each time they come around. For kids in particular, they offer a sense of belonging and a respite from the often harried, confusing, and troubled world outside their doors. Sometimes traditions are created spontaneously; other times they are re-created from the parents' own childhood family traditions.

But what happens when the theology that is wrapped into a given holiday is no longer relevant, but you still long to celebrate? What happens when parents come from two different religious backgrounds and need to commingle their traditions?

These are some of the many dilemmas faced by Unitarian Universalist parents when it comes to celebrating holidays together as a family. Rather than celebrating only secular holidays and the nonreligious aspects of religious holidays, we can determine what religious holidays mean for us based on our values. Considering what we find meaningful about a holiday can help us decide how to celebrate it.

Christmas, Hanukkah and Winter Solstice

Most Unitarian Universalist families celebrate Christmas in some fashion, even though many do not believe in the unique divinity of Jesus. But elevating the idea of Santa Claus above Jesus seems irreverent—even for those parents who are humanist, agnostic, or atheistic. Unitarian Universalist families who aren't Christian often struggle with how to provide meaning in a holiday that celebrates the birth of Jesus.

For Patty French, a parent from Indiana, a favorite childhood memory was setting up the miniature nativity scene underneath the Christmas tree. On Christmas Eve, her family would gather round to hear the story of the baby born in the stable in Bethlehem. Now more of a theist than a Christian, Patty wondered how she could re-create this special magic for her own children despite the change in her theology. Then she hit on the idea of telling the story of how this special baby reminds us that all babies carry inside them the spark of the divine. Here the story represents the hope and promise that all new life brings. Celebrating Christmas as a time of hope and possibilities during the darkest, coldest days of winter can offer families a chance to recognize the power of renewal and affirm the potential in all of us.

The Santa Claus myth also presents a dilemma for some Unitarian Universalist parents who question the ethics of misleading our children in the expectation of material gain. Tom Flynn, author of the essay "The Question of the Claus—Should the Santa Story Stay or Go in Secular Families?" believes that perpetuating the Santa myth discourages critical thinking in children. He says, "Questioning Santa is the first attempt at critical thinking many children make. Yet parents often smokescreen curious children for asking why there are so many Santas at the mall or wondering why Santa and Aunt Nell use the same wrapping paper."

Robin Brzozowski, a parent from Texas, says that by telling our children that Santa Claus is real, "we would be lying to them and teaching them to believe in a mythical magic man who grants your material wishes and to 'just have faith' in something that defies rational explanation." Robin remembers how angry she was when she found out the truth about Santa on the school playground and isn't sure she wants to continue the tradition with her own children.

Some parents may want to avoid perpetuating the Santa myth but not spoil it for other families. "Fairly early, we began explaining to Tanya that Santa was sort of a game that parents played with their children to get more fun out of the holiday season," explains parent Leo Nagorski. "And we explained to her that, because we didn't want to ruin the game for the little ones, we shouldn't go around 'proclaiming' that Santa doesn't exist until the other children and parents are ready."

Other parents use Santa as a metaphor or symbol of the spirit of giving around the Christmas holiday. As Eva Merrell, another parent, explains, "I believe that as our kids get older, we can ease them out of literally believing these myths while still believing in and acting upon the more important lessons."

The overt commercialization of Christmas can also be an issue for families. Many parents are finding value in moving toward a simple Christmas tradition, without a focus on materialism. For although children may jump up and down at the thought of some thrilling new toy, what they most want is quality time spent with loved ones. These moments of family togetherness, not material acquisitions, are the lasting memories that inspire love of the holiday for many years to come. Besides, when the celebration of Christmas focuses on materialism, it can create more financial hardship and stress for those families already struggling to make ends meet.

For some families, deciding whether to celebrate Hanukkah or Christmas or both can become a serious issue. Parents may be concerned that the Jewish tradition will take a backseat to Christmas, and as a result, their children's Jewish heritage may be viewed as second-best. However, as Ron Wolfson explains in his book *Hanukkah*, "Hanukkah cannot hold a candle to Christmas. . . . It is a minor event in the Jewish holiday cycle and has never, until recently, been viewed as a central celebration for the Jewish people." Wolfson suggests that parents wishing to honor their Jewish heritage should emphasize the importance of their High Holy Days and the many minor festivals throughout the year.

Celebrating the winter solstice has been growing in popularity with many families who long for an alternative to Christmas. The solstice celebration honors the human experience; it also celebrates our planet earth and its journey around the sun. My husband and I decided to start celebrating the winter solstice after my then four-year-old daughter asked us why we didn't celebrate Christmas. After some research, we discovered that many sights and symbols of the Christian holiday actually had their roots in pagan celebrations of light around the solstice. Our celebration has evolved over the years and now revolves around the idea of not using electricity after sunset except for heating. Using candles to illuminate our home helps us to remember what it was like for people before electric lights were invented, and how having such long, dark nights might have affected our family's ancestors from northern Europe. We do exchange gifts as part of our family celebration, but we also exchange "wishes." Each family member lights one candle for each of the other members and offers a wish for that person, such as good health, self-confidence, or acceptance.

Other Unitarian Universalist families have celebrated the winter solstice through gatherings of friends to share community on the longest, darkest night of the year. Such opportunities for coming together remind us that we are not alone on our parenting journey and that good friends are important for the nurturing of our souls and deepest selves.

Easter and Passover

Some non-Christian parents who have no problem celebrating Christmas and the birth of Jesus will balk at a holiday commemorating his resurrection. They may concentrate on celebrating the secular elements of the Easter holiday. But since the Easter Bunny, like Santa Claus, is often associated with gifts and candy, other parents may want to downplay this aspect of the holiday or avoid observing it altogether. Meanwhile, Christian Unitarian Universalists may also minimize the treats and sweets in order to honor the religious significance of the day.

The other primary tradition associated with the secular celebration of Easter is the coloring of Easter eggs. This tradition comes from ancient pagan celebrations that heralded the arrival of spring. Eggs have long been associated with new life and were an essential part of spring celebrations in many cultures. Therefore, families who want to celebrate the secular aspects of Easter can consider that they are really commemorating the arrival of spring through the symbols of ancient pagan traditions. Parents can talk about the annual resurrection of life through plants, flowers, and trees. They can encourage their children to color eggs and have egg hunts to celebrate the coming of spring and the changes the earth brings.

The Jewish holiday of Passover also takes place in the spring, although it is not tied to the arrival of the season like Easter. Passover is a time to commemorate and recognize the responsibilities of freedom. The observance lasts eight days, beginning with the Seder, a formal family dinner celebrating the end of the Hebrews' slavery in Egypt. Telling the biblical story of the Exodus from Egypt is a crucial part of the Passover dinner. Yet Passover need not be observed only by the devout. Many secular Jewish families, even those who never or rarely attend synagogue, celebrate Passover together to honor their heritage. Unitarian Universalist families with Jewish roots who choose to honor this heritage through Passover can do so without concerns over a possible theological conflict.

Rosh Hashanah and Yom Kippur

The High Holy Days are indisputably the most important of all Jewish holidays. Rosh Hashanah, often called the Jewish New Year, is celebrated as a time of family gatherings and special meals, but also introspection and reflection. Celebrants are encouraged to look back on the past year and contemplate changes for the year to come. Yom Kippur is observed nine days after Rosh Hashanah. Also known as the Day of Atonement, it is a time of reflection and fasting. Yet how can we reconcile this seeking of forgiveness—this process of actively and intentionally examining one's sins—if we do not believe it is possible to sin or seek forgiveness from a divine presence?

You may find it useful to come up with a ritual that serves a similar purpose of recognizing wrongdoings and beginning the process of healing from them. Such observances might involve many of the same elements as Yom Kippur—fasting, verbal repentance, and confessions that recognize wrongdoings in the hopes of receiving forgiveness. Or you might consider a ritual in which each person takes a turn speaking aloud something done over the past year that was sorrowful or caused regret. Then each person either lights a candle or drops a stone in a bowl of water and speaks about a joy that happened over the past year—perhaps something he or she had done that was particularly meaningful.

Halloween

Recently Halloween has come under fire from diverse groups of people, for very different reasons. On the one hand, evangelical and fundamentalist Christians increasingly protest that Halloween celebrates Satan and all things evil. On the other hand is a plethora of groups who are concerned that many Halloween costumes perpetuate negative stereotypes. Some pagan groups take offense at the way witches are portrayed in costumes and Halloween decorations. Other groups—representing Chinese Americans, Latinos, Native Americans, and others—have also protested pejorative stereotypical costumes. Even the National Alliance on Mental Illness recently has tried to educate people about stereotypes perpetuated by costumes of psycho killers in straitjackets.

By participating in costume selection, you can help your child avoid images that might be offensive. In fact, the process of choosing a Halloween costume can become an exercise in understanding stereotypes and why they are hurtful.

Another concern when it comes to youth and costumes (particularly for females) is the recent trend toward outfits that are revealing and erotic. Nurse outfits which include garter belts and extremely short skirts, fairy tale character costumes which are sexualized, and even "trampy" angels are all the rage for young women. It may even be difficult these days to find a costume for a teenage girl which is not inappropriately sexualized. This hyper-sexualization of costumes for women and young girls perpetuates negative stereotypes—not only in the eyes of the men and boys who will witness them, but also for the girls and young women who will wear them.

Thanksgiving

The annual federal Thanksgiving holiday was set aside to express gratitude for material and spiritual possessions. Most people cele-brate this day with a rather secular gathering of family and friends to share a bountiful feast. However, many feel that the mythology surrounding the First Thanksgiving paints a distorted picture of relations between the colonists and the Wampanoag. Certainly this story ignores the ensuing years of violence and discrimination against Native Americans. Despite many teachers and principals undergoing multicultural and diversity training, negative stereo-types of Native Americans are often perpetuated during lessons and celebrations of Thanksgiving at school.

As recently as 2006, Mindy Whisenhunt, a Unitarian Univer-salist parent, was horrified when her youngest child came home from school with the lyrics for a song she was supposed to memo-rize for a Thanksgiving school play. Mindy felt the lyrics were insensitive and harmful. Despite her fears of the backlash that might result, Mindy summoned the courage to confront the school about the issue. Unfortunately, her six-year-old didn't understand why she didn't get to be in the play while everyone else did. But Mindy felt it was important to hold on to her principles. She hopes that in time her daughter will come to understand her decision.

Beyond the cultural stereotypes often found in the Thanks-giving story, some parents who do not hold a belief in a divine pres-ence aren't sure how to celebrate a holiday that has gratitude at its core. How can we be thankful, they wonder, when there is no one to be thankful to? But whatever one's theology, gratitude can be expressed toward fellow travelers on this planet earth, including the animals that gave their lives for the feast, the persons who prepared the food, and the workers whose salaries allowed for the purchase of the food. Having such a sense of gratitude increases appreciation for what we have, helps us find greater meaning in the present moment, and connects us to the universe.

Martin Luther King Jr. Day

Some secular holidays are particularly relevant to our Unitarian Universalist Principles. We can claim these holidays as particularly meaningful to our faith, and if we choose to do so, add a religious element to them.

One such holiday is Martin Luther King Jr. Day. In addition to celebrating Dr. King's life, it is considered a national day of service—a day of volunteering to feed the hungry, rehabilitate housing, tutor those who can't read, mentor at-risk youngsters, or engage in any of a thousand other projects for building the beloved community of Dr. King's dream.

Even if your family does not engage in social action projects together on this day, the holiday presents an opportunity for children to learn about the power of nonviolent protest and civil disobedience, two key movements of our religious heritage. Unitarian Universalist parent Laura Yamashita marches in the Martin Luther King Jr. parade with her family every year. Through the years, this tradition has made a clear statement to her children about the importance of honoring Dr. King and his work for nonviolent social change.

Earth Day

Earth Day highlights the values espoused by our seventh Principle, "respect for the interdependent web of all existence of which we are a part." Although we strive to be "green" every day, Earth Day is a time to celebrate those efforts and our connections to the earth. We acknowledge the gains we have made in the areas of conservation and environmental protection, but also how far we have yet to go. We recognize that we all play a part in the process and unite around actions to improve our planetary home. Parents can commemorate Earth Day by engaging in local celebrations or participating in intentional efforts as a family: cleaning up a local park, creating art or useful objects out of disposable items, or planting a tree.

John Murray Day

Sometimes it seems as if the only religious holidays we Unitarian Universalists celebrate derive from some other tradition. How can we build Unitarian Universalist identity in our children if all we do is convert the holidays of other faiths into ones we can support and believe in? To fill the need for uniquely Unitarian Universalist celebrations, some families and congregations choose to celebrate John Murray Day.

On or near September 30 of each year, some Unitarian Universalist families celebrate the arrival of John Murray on the New Jersey shore, and hence the arrival of Universalism in America. The story is told that after Murray's ship became stranded on a sandbar, he met a man named Thomas Potter, who was looking for a minister for a church he had just built. Potter asked Murray to preach in his church. Murray—who hoped that the winds would soon change and allow his ship to leave—finally agreed, but only conditionally. "If I'm still here on Sunday," he said, "I will preach."

On Sunday, September 30, the winds had not yet changed, and so Murray did preach a sermon in Potter's church. His Universalist message of a loving God who would not damn anyone to hell was welcome news in America. Soon Murray found himself preaching regularly to larger and larger crowds up and down the northeastern seaboard.

Families can celebrate John Murray Day by flying a kite or going sailing (to celebrate the power of wind), by having a celebratory dinner (like the one at which Potter asked Murray to preach), or by placing stones in a waterfall or fountain to redirect the flow of water (symbolizing how a seemingly simple event can change everything).

Realistic Expectations

Family pressures are sometimes exaggerated during the holidays, particularly those that occur during the winter season. Our society not only emphasizes consumerism, but also offers unrealistic expectations through commercials, TV specials, and movies. Many families feel disappointment and anxiety when their own family time is not as wonderful as what is portrayed in the media. Instead of reacting to societal pressures, you can be responsible for your own expectations during the holidays and help your family be responsible for theirs. Decide as a family what is important, and let go of the events and activities that cause special stress or unfulfilled expectations.

For single parents or families struggling with financial issues, the stress and strain of the holidays can be daunting. When even the gift of time spent together is difficult to provide, parents can suffer from guilt or regret. Likewise, blended families or families who are separated by divorce or military service have to contend with the whereabouts of family members during the holidays and the feelings of isolation, loneliness, and sadness for parents and children who will spend holidays apart.

When a family is dealing with the pain and grief of having lost someone important to them, the holidays can seem even more overwhelming. Holiday traditions bring up many memories— some good, some bad. Taking time to acknowledge these losses is the first step toward healing. Don't try to use your celebrations to compensate for these losses, or you will find yourself continually disappointed. Instead, look for ways to affirm where you are and who you are with right now by creating new celebrations or reinventing meaningful traditions.

For many families, another source of holiday pressure is the feeling of being pulled in multiple directions. Trying to accommodate the expectations and traditions of extended family and friends may leave little opportunity for you and your children to celebrate in your own way. If you have older children or youth, enlist their aid in considering what is special about the holidays and how best to celebrate them together. You may decide to spend a quiet holiday at home and visit extended family on other days. Or you may choose to spend major holidays with a wider circle of family or friends and set aside other special times for your immediate family to be together.

Spiritual Practices

Expressing your spirituality is a way of connecting with your soul, your innermost spark, the deepest part of yourself. Any avenue that gets you to that point can be considered a spiritual practice. Thinking about the variety of spiritual practices that are possible and experimenting with some of them is a way to find something meaningful for the whole family—or at least for one parent and one child. It may be that one child really connects with meditation and mindfulness, while another prefers a more physically active method of expressing spirituality, such as yoga, tai chi, or the martial arts. As parents, we do not need to require that our children express their spiritual selves in the same way we do; instead, we should model the value of engaging in spiritual practices and help our children discover that which is meaningful for them.

Still, educators of all religious traditions emphasize that a child's attitude toward spirituality will ultimately derive from the parents. Therefore, the spiritual practices you introduce to your children will impact their lifelong view of spiritual expression. For this reason, it makes sense to pursue practices that reflect your own personal theological beliefs and the type of spirituality you would like your children to experience.

Not all of the spiritual practices explored in this chapter will be meaningful to you or your family; nor are they meant to be. Unitarian Universalists are theologically diverse, but even more diverse when it comes to expressing spirituality. While some find their moments of connection in nature, others prefer practices that expand the mind through inspiration such as reading sacred texts or discovering new scientific information, and still others prefer sensory or physical experiences.

Children often express their spirituality most naturally with their physical selves, particularly those who are kinesthetic learners. Watch children running with abandon, inspired to propel their bodies as fast as they are physically able, and you catch a glimpse of true, uninhibited bliss.

Just the simple act of caring for one's body also has a spiritual dimension to it. Scott Alexander, in *Everyday Spiritual Practice*, points out that a practice of regular exercise "can be a discipline of spiritual self-care that naturally leads to spiritual other-care, and thus to right relation with all you encounter and touch." For this reason, this chapter includes several forms of physical exercise that can be powerful spiritual practices as well.

It is important to remember—particularly when it comes to adolescents—that what may be a meaningful spiritual experience for you may not resonate with your youth. A teenager may long to experiment with New Age or mystical spiritual practices that could be disconcerting to a humanist or agnostic parent. Likewise, pagan parents may feel disappointment that their adolescent no longer wants to participate in sacred rituals and theistic or Christian parents may feel disappointment when their teen rejects reciting bedtime prayers. There is a strong possibility that the two of you will need to express your spirituality differently. There's nothing wrong with that—only opportunities for both of you to explore some of the many possibilities that are available.

Martial Arts

Martial arts training is often recommended for active children who need an outlet for their energy and a way to learn self-discipline. Some adults begin martial arts training with the goal of self-defense. Many people soon discover that the martial arts are really more than this—they can be a form of spiritual practice.

The martial arts are physical and mental disciplines that cultivate a particular attitude of awareness, harmony, and nonviolence. In fact, children and youth are taught specifically that they should never use their martial arts training aggressively.

Most martial arts have roots in the religious traditions of Buddhism, Confucianism, and Taoism. There are a variety of martial arts to choose from, and many different styles within each, depending on which country the art developed in and what kind of focus it takes.

Tae kwon do originated in Korea. Its name is loosely translated as "the way of the foot and the fist." Modern forms of tae kwon do usually emphasize control and self-defense, with an emphasis on kicks using the greater reach and power of the leg (as opposed to the arm).

Karate, probably the most familiar of the martial arts, originated in Japan. It is primarily a striking art, using punches, kicks, knee and elbow strikes, and open-handed techniques rather than fists. Modern karate programs emphasize self-development, perseverance, virtue, and leadership.

Jujitsu, which literally means "the art of softness," evolved from the principle of using the attacker's energy against him. This form involves throwing and pinning rather than striking and kicking. Judo, which evolved from jujitsu, also emphasizes immobilizing rather than hitting.

Aikido can be translated as "the way of unifying with life energy." It is performed by blending with the attacker and redirecting the force of the attack rather than opposing it head-on. Morihei Ueshiba, the founder of aikido, explained the intent when he said, "To control aggression without inflicting injury is the art of peace."

Tai chi (also known as tai chi chuan) is considered a "soft" martial art. It arose in China as a system of self-defense that emphasized meeting force with softness, safely redirecting the force and thereby reducing or eliminating injury. Today tai chi is more often practiced for its health benefits than for self-defense. Most people recognize it as a series of choreographed movements, often performed as a group, to regulate the flow of *chi*, or energy force, within the body.

Despite the emphasis on self-defense, all quality martial arts programs go beyond the physical and aim to develop the whole individual. As Rev. Sarah Lammert explains in her essay in *Everyday Spiritual Practice*, "The martial arts for me embody the unity of heart, mind, and body. There are slow, spiral movements that look like leaves floating down into a pond; there are sharp, stinging movements that mimic fierce animals; there are powerful, sly balancing acts that require lightness and strength in the same moment." Learning what is known as "forms"—a series of formalized, sequenced moves against an imaginary opponent—is an essential part of most martial arts programs. These forms are choreographed, and when performed they appear like an elaborate dance. During the exercise, participants are engaged in a meditative state as they move through the flowing sequence.

While some of us may have trouble getting past the impression of martial arts as fighting, others are discovering the power of channeling anger and energies through these ancient physical and mental disciplines. For my adolescent daughter, tae kwon do has brought not only a greater sense of physical awareness and power, but also focus and emotional clarity. The sparring gives her a positive outlet for her aggression, and orchestrating the forms has allowed this girl, who struggled with gymnastics and had little sense of rhythm for dancing, feel coordinated and graceful for the first time in her life. It's also pretty impressive to see her kick as high as her head, particularly when—at age fourteen—she is taller than I am.

Yoga

Yoga, which developed in ancient India, was originally associated with Hinduism. While most practicing Hindus actively engage in yoga poses (*asanas*), and many of the poses have ancient Sanskrit names, yoga now enjoys wide appeal among religions. It has also found its way into secular health clubs as a form of physical exercise that promotes balance and flexibility.

As a physical activity, some styles of yoga are particularly beneficial for those who are unable to participate in vigorous exercise, such as children with asthma. But contrary to what many people think, yoga is more than simply an attempt to twist the body into the shape of a pretzel. The poses, in combination with breathing techniques, can help bring focus and spiritual energy into one's life. What many of us in the West consider yoga is really only one facet of an entire regimen or lifestyle promoting balance, harmony, and centeredness.

A regular yoga practice can help children develop calmness, confidence, and self-discipline. The poses sharpen the ability to focus the mind, particularly when children are encouraged to think about what the postures mean and transform themselves into those images—strong and confident like a warrior, or playful like a dog doing a bow for attention. Yoga has even been shown to help children diagnosed with attention deficit hyperactivity disorder, who crave movement and an abundance of sensorimotor stimuli, by channeling these impulses in a positive way.

Adolescents may feel a lesser need to exert themselves physically than younger children, but the self-discipline and focus of yoga can provide an anchor in the chaos that is often their life. Yoga can help them improve not only their physical balance, but their emotional and spiritual balance. Youth can engage in the breathing, meditation, and relaxation techniques that are often a part of yoga practice, thereby deepening the experience of connection with the body.

There are many varieties of yoga. Some of them consist of a series of fluid or static postures (*asanas*) and breath control (*pranayama*) and are what most people think of as yoga. Other forms are more physically vigorous, aiming to burn calories and build muscle as practitioners become more flexible in body and spirit. Forms of "hot" yoga involve sweating during the poses to promote the release of body toxins. Still other forms of yoga are deeply mystical, involving chanting and loud breathing while holding the poses. Most varieties of yoga emphasize healthy, nonviolent ways of living, breath and energy pathways, meditation, and self-reflection. Once you decide what you and your family members want out of the practice, you can seek out a teacher or school that practices the form of yoga you prefer.

Nature Walks

Many Unitarian Universalists describe walking in nature as their preferred spiritual practice. With intentionality and purpose, such walks can deepen the spiritual lives of family members.

Even a casual walk in a forest allows us to feel connected to the natural world, and this connection often brings a sense of peace and centering. Regular family walks with the intention of communing with nature can offer families a sense of touching the sacred, of recognizing our place in the wider universe.

However, parents can easily become frustrated when their vision of a peaceful walk through nature clashes with the reality of comments like "This is boring," or youngsters darting about with great energy but seemingly little sense of purpose. The key is to keep the length of the walk short and age-appropriate. (For more information on making nature hikes meaningful for children, see the chapter "The Interdependent Web.")

Encourage youth to walk in silence, intensifying the experience through absorption in the sights, sounds, and smells of the nature walk. Invite them to share their impressions after the walk is over. You may be amazed at what they experience and how they express it.

Nature connections don't have to be limited to hikes in forests. Seeing trees growing haphazardly out of rocky outcrops carved thousands of years ago by receding glaciers, exploring the darkness of deep underground caves and understanding what true silence is, feeling the heat of the sun while walking through the desert—all are ways we can experience a spiritual tie to the earth. Anytime we experience the wonder of the natural world, we can't help but be reminded of how we are just a minuscule part of this interdependent web of life on our planet.

In an urban environment, nature often takes a back seat to the wonders that humans have created. However, it is still possible to engage in meditative walks through city parks and nearby nature preserves. When access to green grass and trees is limited in our area, we can still benefit from walking together and feeling the connections of the world around us, perhaps by tuning in to the many sights and sounds of our environment, which otherwise may go unnoticed because of its familiarity.

Labyrinths

An ancient symbol that refers to wholeness, the labyrinth has long been used as a vehicle for walking meditations and centering. Combining the imagery of the circle and the spiral, a meandering but purposeful path is laid out representing a spiritual journey to the very center of ourselves and then back out again into the world.

Labyrinths are sometimes confused with mazes. A maze is like a puzzle and may contain twists, turns, and dead ends. It requires us to use logic to form a rational plan to find our way out. In contrast, a labyrinth has only one path, and the way in is the same as the way out. Walking a labyrinth involves not the logical, thinking brain, but the passive, emotional, spiritual brain that concentrates on the journey and the experience rather than on finding a solution to a problem.

There is no one right way to walk a labyrinth, even though there is only one path. You can walk a labyrinth with intentional self-reflection on the present moment, or you can imagine it as representing your entire life journey in miniature. You can focus on the turns and curves of the labyrinth, or you can reflect on how the path seems to circle back to the places you were before, but only coming close without actually crossing them.

Labyrinths can be walked in a solemn, contemplative manner or in celebration and joy. Children seem to instinctively sense the celebratory aspect and often want to take off running. Try giving children musical instruments to play, scarves to wave, or bubbles to blow as you traverse the path with them. Using props like these helps children slow down and adults speed up, so that both young and old are in nearly the same place.

Many congregations have added labyrinths to their grounds as more of their members learn to appreciate this spiritual practice. If there are no labyrinths near you, consider traveling to visit one as a pilgrimage of sorts. Treating the labyrinth as a special destination will make the experience even more memorable for the family. You could also make plans to visit a labyrinth while on a vacation or weekend trip.

Once you are familiar with the basic pattern of a labyrinth, it is easy to create one anywhere there is enough space. The amount of space needed depends primarily on how wide you want the paths to be. Ideally, the path should be wide enough so that two people going in opposite directions can pass each other easily.

Stone is often used as a building material for permanent outdoor labyrinths, but many other materials can be used. Labyrinths have been mowed into grass or marked out with masking tape in a meeting room cleared of tables and chairs.

Even if there is no labyrinth nearby and no space to create one, it is still possible to experience the power of a labyrinth without traveling. You can "walk" a miniature labyrinth with your finger. Scale models and pictures are available on the Internet, either free or for purchase. Focusing on the movements of your finger through the miniature path can offer many of the same benefits as walking a full-scale labyrinth. Tracing the path can bring peace to your soul and harmony to your inner self. It can provide spiritual balance as you journey into the center and back out again.

Meditation

As a way to promote emotional healing and a deeper awareness of both the self and the world, many Unitarian Universalists find meditation to be an enriching experience. For some, prayer functions as meditation. For others, meditation takes the place of prayer.

Although meditation is most closely associated with Buddhism and Hinduism, some form of the practice is utilized by every major religion of the world. In Western traditions, the term *contemplative prayer* refers to practices very similar to meditation in Eastern traditions. In addition, the rosary used by Catholics in prayer serves as a meditative process. The spoken prayers follow a specific order, much like a mantra. Fingers hold the rosary beads which, like the prayer beads used by some Buddhists, serve to focus the mind. The size and shape of the beads, their smooth surfaces, and the rhythmic clicking as they are pressed against one another offer a sense of peace and centering. The bodily movement in Muslim prayer is also meditative in nature, since it involves a series of repetitive movements and words. Engaging in these repetitive acts relaxes the body and centers the mind, promoting a deeper emotional state and spiritual awareness.

The benefits of meditation are many. A calm and centered mind allows a person to focus and work through problems step by step. Meditation helps reduce the fight-or-flight reflex that occurs during times of stress. It has also been proven to reduce overall stress levels and aid in healing. Meditation can increase our sense of tranquility, as we learn to be aware of emotions like anger or sadness and yet experience inner peace in spite of these feelings. And as Jane Bartlett tells us in *Parenting with Spirit*, meditation "can help us to experience the interconnectedness of the world, and compassion and love for everyone and everything around us."

Engaging in meditative practices with children invites the calming of a child's body and mind. Meditation can help children learn to concentrate, encourage positive self-talk, and build confidence. The regular use of meditation teaches children a useful technique for dealing with anxiety and stress, one that they can rely on to help them through difficult times and life challenges. Above all, meditation is a practice of self-discovery and self-expression that can also help move us beyond the ordinariness of life to touch the greater mystery.

As Kerry Solomon writes in an article in *Spiritual Mothering Journal*, "Sixty seconds of stillness may easily seem like an hour to a young person. It's no small accomplishment to achieve that." Learning through practice and effort that they can quiet themselves for a brief period of time can be a powerful experience for children. And it is not just children who struggle with quieting the mind and body. Says Solomon, "Silence frightens a lot of people. Traditional prayers let you know where you stand: there are words learned by heart or written in a book to define your innermost thoughts. Quiet can be dark formlessness." The real value of meditation is in this process of focusing inward—quieting the mind in order to escape the chaos of whirling thoughts that characterizes so much of daily life.

Preschool children will readily take to meditation if it is presented in a simple, low-key manner. When teaching meditation to children, keep these tips in mind:

- *Eliminate possible distractions.* Find a quiet, peaceful time and place to meditate, away from other family members, TV, music, toys, and any other items that have the potential to distract.

- *Establish sacred time and space.* This is crucial so that your child learns that meditation is what is done in this place and time. Some parents create an altar with special stones, candles, a fountain, or other meaningful objects. Meditating at an established time of day helps your child learn expectations for the ritual.

- *Assume comfortable positions.* Eliminating stray thoughts from your mind is tough enough without the distraction of having an uncomfortable body. You and your child might sit on cushions on the floor with legs crossed, or in chairs with your backs straight and feet flat on the floor. Lying down is not recommended, since it encourages sleep rather than meditation—unless sleeping is the desired result, such as when meditating just before the child's bedtime.

- *Keep your sessions short.* The younger the child, the shorter the sessions need to be. Probably the best you can hope for is one minute per year of age. Children who have been meditating for some time can achieve better results than beginners, but still, the shorter the better.

- *Engage in the practice regularly.* There is a reason why it is called "the practice of meditation." It requires practice, practice, and more practice. To truly get comfortable with meditation, both children and adults need to do it regularly and frequently.

Anne Carson, in *Spiritual Parenting In a New Age*, suggests that simple relaxation and centering exercises are probably sufficient for the first few years. Once the child has shown interest in and an aptitude for meditation, some practice in guided imagery and visualizations can be added.

Compared to younger children, teenagers are much more capable of keeping their bodies still. However, they may have an even harder time keeping their minds quieted, particularly if they are new to meditation. Today's youth are highly skilled at filling up their minds—with music, instant messaging, TV, and computer games. Meditation requires the opposite of multitasking, which may seem foreign and uncomfortable at first. However, given time and repeated efforts, they can learn to quiet their minds.

When teaching meditation to adolescents, the same basic guidelines apply as for younger children. It is also important for teens to be self-motivated and to choose a time and place that works for them. Studies have shown that teens tend to be much more alert in the evening than in the morning. Trying to get your teen to meditate when she would much rather be sleeping is likely to be fruitless.

Start by helping teens concentrate on their breathing, focusing on each breath as it is inhaled and released. Encourage them to try making their inhalations the same length as their exhalations. If they need more concentration to focus, invite them to imagine breathing in peace and breathing out chaos.

Help teens understand that it will be difficult to keep their minds focused on their breath. Encourage them to take notice and acknowledge any thoughts that arise, gently noticing where their attention has been drawn, and then allowing the breath to again become predominant. Sometimes it is helpful to acknowledge, "That's a thought," and then go back to concentrating on breathing once again.

As parents, we can encourage our teens to remember that quiet doesn't have to equal bored or asleep or even deep thinking. By helping them connect to the extraordinary experiences that can happen as part of everyday life, we may be able to reawaken their sense of wonder. The teen years are often when we learn to squelch our yearning for magic in life, and when wide-eyed wonder is no longer considered acceptable behavior. For this reason, Mimi Doe says in *10 Principles for Spiritual Parenting*, teens have to turn off their ever-present internal critic in order to fully experience meditation or mindfulness. Encouraging our youth to ignore that inner critic and tune in to their deeper selves can be our gift to them.

Modeling the practice of meditation in your own life communicates its value and sets a good example for your teenager. This is true when it comes to most any spiritual practice that you would like your child to experience. Even if you do not regularly pursue meditation as a spiritual practice yourself, if your child or teen approaches you and asks for your help in learning meditation, you can be supportive and provide assistance in the way that feels most comfortable to you.

Prayer

Because meditation and prayer are so closely intertwined, it is sometimes difficult to distinguish between the two. While some Unitarian Universalists find greater meaning with one practice than the other, many find some value in both these spiritual practices and desire to share them with their children.

Prayer serves many different functions and, depending on how and when it is used, offers different benefits to those who practice it. Spoken prayer can be the ritual repetition of a brief phrase, or the saying of a traditional rote prayer—these affirm the meaning of those words in the consciousness of the person praying. Spoken prayer can also be more open-ended, allowing for the free expression of thoughts. Contemplative prayer, on the other hand, is the Western term for meditation—a silent emptying of oneself to bring greater awareness of the interior life and our connection to the mysteries of existence.

If you were raised without prayer or have negative associations with the word, then you may feel reluctant to engage in this spiritual practice or encourage it in your children. However, prayer has benefits that make it worth considering. It helps children—and adults—feel connected to a larger reality. Whether you and your child think of that larger reality as a divine presence, Great Spirit, the universe, or the greater humanity, connection to this larger reality affirms your place in this world and offers some meaning about where you fit within the scheme of things.

According to Jane Bartlett in *Parenting with Spirit*, prayer can also be considered a way to expand our consciousness and suspend ordinary thought. This process can be useful in touching the deepest self, when our logical minds are shut off and we allow our spiritual voices to be heard. In this way, prayer promotes inner reflection. Since so many of our thoughts remain "under the surface" yet affect our behavior, having some time to tie into that part of ourselves can be useful and even healing.

Prayer can also promote self-awareness. This is particularly true of open-ended prayers that offer blessings to the people who are important to us or of words of gratitude for the good things in life. Having times to regularly express their interior experience stimulates this self-awareness in children. By attending to their emotions and processing them, children and youth may begin to understand the feelings they experience and either accept them or resolve to change them. In this way, prayer can be not only a tool for developing self-awareness, but an act of transformation.

Spoken prayers that repeat the same words time and again can serve a meditative function in the life of a child, providing focus and honing the mind. They may also serve as a source of comfort for many years beyond childhood. The embedding of prayers in the hearts and minds of our children can be part of the gift we pass down to them.

However, the simple recitation of rote prayers is not enough. The meaning of the words must be understood by children and be relevant to their lives. Children's minds often make odd links between what they do and don't understand, and they have a tendency to "fill in the gaps" where they find holes. If they misunderstand the words of a prayer, they may come up with a meaning quite different from the one intended.

Prayers for children must also reflect a healthy, affirming theology consistent with their family's beliefs. Be thoughtful about the prayers you use with children, beginning with honest reflection about your own theological understanding.

For those who believe in a divine presence, prayers of gratitude and praise encourage deep feelings of reverence. However, even families that do not recognize a higher power can use prayers of gratitude to express appreciation for everyday events and to recognize the specialness of life. These prayers can be especially powerful when children offer up their own words of thanks as a genuine expression of what is in their hearts. Encourage your child to express his gratitude each day, perhaps as part of a bedtime or mealtime ritual. You might start by mentioning something you are grateful for, then invite your child to do the same. Or you could teach your child some opening words to start her prayers, such as "The gifts I have are many—I am grateful for . . ." or "Now at the end of the day, I pause to remember what I am grateful for . . ."

Laura Riney, a parent from Illinois, lights a battery-operated candle at night while she and her son say their bedtime blessing—a hybrid of rote prayer and open-ended prayer that she invented when her son Rowan was a baby. She used to sing it to him, but now that he is older, he says it along with her. Their prayer begins, "Blessings on this day, blessings on this night. May the angels guard us and keep us in their light." Then she and her son ask for blessings on people in their life. The prayer ends with ". . . and God bless all of our family and all of our friends. May the angel's light shine upon them. Amen."

For some families, prayers of concern for others are also important. Even those parents who feel there is no presence to petition for healing or protection can teach their children the value of praying for others. Scientific studies have shown that the belief that one is being prayed for offers some healing and strength to get through the malady. Simply knowing that others are concerned can serve as a powerful healing force.

Mimi Doe suggests that parents encourage their children to think of a person they care for very much, perhaps a sick person who needs healing or another child who is going through a difficult time, and send light or love to that person. Doe writes, "Tell them to visualize this light forming a bridge and flood the person at the other end with good feelings, health, and strength of spirit." Or children might visualize this healing light enveloping the other person in an embrace of comfort.

Even moments of deliberate, focused silence, in lieu of mealtime or bedtime prayers, can be powerful in helping children and youth to pause, pay attention, and focus on something greater than themselves. Whether it takes the form of sitting in silence, repeating familiar words, or sharing deep personal feelings, prayer can be healing and transformative.

Chanting

An ancient spiritual technique for stilling the mind and invoking one's higher self, chanting may be connected with yoga or meditation or serve as a spiritual practice in its own right. Chanting may simply be the rhythmic speaking of words, or it may be more like a song. Concentrating on reproducing the sound of the chant, as well as regulating the breath, goes beyond meditation to invoke a deep physical and sensory response.

Chants are a path to spiritual development in many religious traditions. Chanting can be found in ancient and modern Native

American ceremonies, tribal traditions of Africa, the Gregorian chants of Christian monks, and some Qur'anic readings. Chanting is an integral part of many Buddhist traditions and is essential to Hindu spiritual practices.

The concept behind chanting is that sometimes mere speech cannot take us where we wish to go. Chanting is another way of shutting off the thinking, logical brain and tuning into the emotional or spiritual side of ourselves. Chanting often involves the use of mantras—words and sounds that vibrate at the highest levels of awareness. Chanting a mantra is said to still and open the mind, dissolve worries, and help us touch the sacred, whatever that may be.

Hindus consider the Sanskrit word *om* (pronounced "ohm") as the primal sound that contains all other sounds, much as white light encompasses all colors of the spectrum. Using this word as a chant is believed to have mind-stilling qualities for both adults and children. Doe suggests that you encourage your children to concentrate on the "om" sound as it is chanted—the way it echoes and vibrates throughout their entire bodies. Encourage them to feel the sound in their chests, in their throats, and in their hearts. Doe even says you can invite your children to visualize the way om looks and to try to "see" its form as it leaves their mouths.

Another commonly chanted word is *peace* or its Sanskrit version, *shanti*. While the latter perhaps carries greater beauty and mystery, the simple word *peace* has great meaning for Unitarian Universalists and is understood by even the youngest children.

Several short songs in the Unitarian Universalist hymnal, *Singing the Living Tradition*, work well as chants. They include "Hineh Mah Tov," and "Hava Nashirah," both in Hebrew with English translations; "Jubilate Deo," in Latin; "Sing and Rejoice"; "The Earth, Water, Fire, Air"; and "Gathered Here."

Tarot Cards

Associated with fortune tellers and crystal balls, tarot cards are often dismissed as a carnival sideshow. But while they may not predict the future, they can crystallize our thoughts about what the future may hold by encouraging personal reflection and self-examination.

Children in particular, when given an accepting environment, can be incredibly attuned to their own intuitive perceptions. Many of us lose this ability as we mature, learning to rely more on our logical brains and rejecting the intuitive parts of ourselves. Because of their pictorial and symbolic nature, tarot cards help us tap into that intuition, and in the case of children, may help them to hone their skills so they never lose them.

Most tarot decks consist of a pack of seventy-eight cards divided into the major and minor arcana. The twenty-two major arcana cards symbolize key life events, lessons, or growth phases. These cards are usually full of esoteric symbols that trigger intuitive responses and are the most recognizable of the cards from a cultural perspective. For instance, the hanged man and the death card are both major arcana cards.

The minor arcana cards are similar to a regular playing card deck, consisting of four suits (wands, pentacles, swords, and cups) that range from ace to king. It is generally accepted that wands symbolize growth, pentacles stand for wealth or material goods, swords symbolize pain and sorrow, and cups stand for happiness, love, and joy.

Young children can sort the cards, grouping them however they wish. They can also pick a card and tell a story about what the card means from their perspective. Older children can pick two or three cards and tell a story that unites them into a narrative. Older children and teens can also begin to use the cards as a tool for insight into their emotional selves. As Gail Fairfield explains in her essay from the book *Spiritual Parenting in a New Age*, if a child is having difficulty describing her feelings, she could look through the cards until she finds one that "speaks" to her. Often, with the tarot as a trigger, she'll be able to talk about what's bothering her.

Creative Expression

Because spirituality comes from our deepest selves and involves the intuitive/emotional brain rather than the thinking/logical brain, there is sometimes a very fine line between spiritual expression and creative expression.

Children are naturals when it comes to expressing their spirituality and their creativity, which for many children may be one and the same. Sometimes all we as parents need to do is provide the necessary materials, then get out of the way and let children follow their passion. Some adults are intimidated by the mess that children's art activities, such as painting, drawing, sculpting, or cutting and pasting, inevitably generate. Others are too deeply mired in their own desires for perfection to see the beauty in what small hands can produce. However, to truly nurture children's artistic souls and spiritual selves, we just need to give them freedom and appreciate their creative endeavors, no matter how much the art critic within ourselves is tempted to teach them "the right way" to do it.

Older children and teens can be very critical of themselves when it comes to spiritual or creative expression. By adolescence, they have usually already decided whether or not they have artistic talent, based on the people around them who have judged their work. If over the years they have been told (or have gotten the impression) that their art is not as good as that of others, they are likely to have trouble letting go and expressing what is truly inside them. Offering alternative methods of artistic expression may be the key to silencing the inner critic. If your son finds drawing too intimidating, working on a collage might free up his creativity. If sculpting is troublesome for your daughter, perhaps an art software program will get her creative juices flowing.

All children are drawn to music. Even young children can thrill to making sounds with simple rhythm instruments or dancing as the spirit moves them. Providing opportunities for children to express their spiritual selves through music doesn't require expensive lessons or even real musical instruments. A wooden spoon and metal pot, or a makeshift guitar fashioned out of a tissue box and rubber bands, may be all a child needs to revel in the wonder of music. If youth continue to pursue music as a spiritual practice, be supportive and offer opportunities for enrichment as you are able. Give them space and time to pursue their love of music, and remind them that they need not be "the best" in order to continue on this spiritual path. Whether or not they eventually become professional musicians, their love of music will continue to nourish their souls for all of their lives, unless this passion is quashed by others who insist on perfection and competition.

Writing is another avenue of creative expression that has close ties to spirituality. For teens in particular, journaling and poetry are ways to express the deep pain and joy that is in their souls. As in other areas of creative expression, offer encouragement without criticism to nurture this spiritual practice. Children of all ages should be encouraged to tell their own stories. Not only does storytelling help children develop their vocabulary and express themselves verbally, it offers them the opportunity to tap into their innermost thoughts, dreams, and hopes in ways that mere discussion could never do.

In fact, all forms of creative expression offer that potential. Whether a person is drawn to the visual arts, the performing arts, or the expressive arts, spiritual development through artistic endeavors is a comfortable way to touch the sacred and release the divine spark that is within each of us.

Mindfulness

Spirituality does not have to be something huge, distant, and elusive. As Nancy Fuchs reminds us in *Our Share of Night, Our Share of Morning*, spirituality can be "tucked within the moments, the ordinary activities of waking, of eating, of going to sleep. Sometimes, we are fortunate enough to notice."

Practicing mindfulness is a way of appreciating life during the moments in which we live them. The intentionality of maintaining awareness of what you are doing at any given moment is a spiritual practice that recognizes that all life is precious and time itself is sacred.

Mindfulness offers parents the opportunity to look past the surface and see our children more clearly as they truly are. Usually we are so busy meeting our obligations and appointments that we are not particularly mindful of what is going on around us. Then one day we look at our children, and it hits us like a blow to the chest—they suddenly seem older, more mature, more like self-reliant individuals and less like our dependent children needing direction and guidance. At times like this, mindful parenting kicks in unbidden, and we are forced to recognize who our children are in the present moment. Experiencing more of these moments by intentionally practicing mindful parenting can be healing and transformative for both children and parents.

However, being mindful is not as easy as it sounds. As Thich Nhat Hahn tells us in *Being Peace*, we have a tendency to postpone being alive to some point in the future. Hahn believes this is because we are not used to being with ourselves; he says we often act as if we don't like ourselves and are trying to escape from ourselves.

On the other hand, children have no such qualms. Young children in particular practice mindfulness in a way adults can only envy. Since they have little past to dwell on, and the future is an abstract concept to them, it is easy for children to simply live in the moment. And yet we do everything we can to get them to hurry up, plan for the future, and think ahead. Despite our frustration with children's focus on the here and now, we can learn something from them about appreciating life while it is lived rather than in retrospect. Sometimes we need to stop on the path and watch the spider spin its web, or pause to revel in the rainbow projected on the ceiling of the living room. Observing the look of pure amazement and wonder on the face of a toddler who is totally engrossed in the object before him, we are reminded that everything is new to him. And seeing the joy on their faces as children run and play freely, we glimpse the true spirit of the present without fears of the future or hang-ups with the past.

In our busy lives, sometimes doing nothing is truly a gift we can give to ourselves, our children, and our partners or spouses. While it may seem as if doing nothing is an unbelievable extravagance, sometimes it can be just the rejuvenation the family needs.

This is the theory behind family vacations, be they be expensive getaways or just time away from the usual routine. Vacations can regenerate our spirits, recharge our batteries, and allow time to be together as a family. If you can avoid overscheduling and allow some flexibility for spontaneous fun, vacations can be just the catalyst to generate the deep reflection that is an essential part of mindful parenting.

However, you don't need to take a family vacation and spend large sums of money to spend time together. Stanley Greenspan, a child psychiatrist at George Washington University Medical School, recommends a technique known as "floor time." He encourages parents to literally sit on the floor with their young children and truly be present with them, without trying to surreptitiously read a magazine article or check things off a mental to-do list. Greenspan says this time should be free of any parental instruction—no teaching the alphabet, counting, or matching. Instead, just follow the child's lead and actively participate without taking charge.

When it comes to older children and teens, "doing nothing" together may mean sprawling on the couch with them, actively listening as they tell you about the book they are reading or the movie they saw. It may mean listening to your teen's music with her, exploring the meaning of the lyrics or the visuals in the video without being judgmental or critical. It may mean just "hanging out" with your adolescent, being present should he wish to confide in you.

As Madeline Levine explains in *The Price of Privilege*, it is during quiet, unpressured moments that youth will expose the most tender parts of their developing selves to their parents. Not taking time to just "be" with your adolescent means less opportunity for deep interaction. And since true, deep sharing comes from an intimate relationship forged over time, it may take many opportunities of just being together, without any agenda or plan, before real communication can occur between the two of you.

If you have a partner on your parenting journey, the two of you also need time away together without your children in order to strengthen your relationship. Scientific evidence confirms that parenting is hard on marital relationships and partnerships. Just as individuals need to nurture their souls and regenerate their energy for parenting, partners need time and attention to rejuvenate their relationship. Reconnecting with one another and sharing intimate moments together can help keep you together through the stress of daily life.

Inherent Worth and Dignity

Our first Unitarian Universalist Principle is sometimes held up as the cornerstone of our faith. Despite our diversity of theology and the myriad of ways in which we explore our spiritual natures, we all generally believe that there is a spark of the holy in every person. This is significant, because many religions hold a different view of the essential nature of humanity.

Mainline Christian theology contends that we were created in the image of God, and that the fall from grace that occurred in the Garden of Eden changed the nature of humanity. The disobedience of Adam and Eve resulted in the concept of universal sin, summarized by the apostle Paul in the Christian Bible as "all have sinned and fall short of the glory of God" and "there is no one who is righteous, not even one."

This view of humanity as inherently sinful is in direct contrast to our first Principle. We believe in the essential goodness of humankind. This idea was inherited in part from our Universalist ancestors, who rejected the idea of a sinful human nature and focused instead on a loving God who offered universal salvation for all people, everywhere. Unitarians also historically accepted that human nature was essentially good, believing that damaging social conditions created the evil behavior prevalent in our world.

This sense of essential goodness translates into a view that we all have the possibility of becoming our best selves, although circumstances and life events may keep us from achieving this potential. It is this life view that we pass on to our children in the hope of raising caring, compassionate, and generous people with an attitude of gratitude and respect for others.

In the various children's versions of our Principles used in religious education programs, the complicated words "inherent worth and dignity" are sometimes replaced with "each and every person is important" or "we respect each person." This is unfortunate, because neither of these re-phrasings quite captures the power of "inherent worth and dignity." As parents, we can reinforce the idea of everyone being important and the value of treating everyone with respect, but we should also remember to lift up the idea of inherent goodness that separates our beliefs from some religious cultures of Christianity. We ought to teach older children and youth the more complicated phrasing and help them understand what we mean by it.

Nurturing Empathy

If we do not respect a person's ideas, beliefs, longings, and dreams, then that person will not feel worthy of dignity. The best way to offer a person respect is through truly listening to what her or she has to say. Truly listening involves empathy and compassion.

Many parents have deep concerns about their children's apparent lack of empathy for others. However, behavioral theorists have determined that physiological changes must take place in the brain before children can understand the perspective of others. As Elizabeth Berger explains in *Raising Kids with Character*, empathy requires children to recognize that they are not the center of the universe. Because children are so egocentric, it is really difficult (or in the case of young children, impossible) for them to understand that someone else has feelings different from their own. It is only with maturity that children can understand that each of us is only a single participant in a shared reality of laws and therefore principles that apply to everyone.

Berger also believes that a child's capacity for empathy cannot blossom when the parent approaches interpersonal conflicts between friends or siblings as legal violations. If a parent continually inter-venes and doles out punishment instead of teaching conflict resolu-tion skills, then children will continue to look to outside sources to solve their conflicts. When we trust that our children have the capacity to develop empathy for others, then we show our children that we have faith in them. (For information on how to communi-cate conflict resolution skills in children and youth, see the chapter "Peace, Liberty and Justice for All.")

Respecting Our Children

Until children are able to empathize on their own, they need to have respect modeled for them. There is no more powerful way to do this than for parents to treat children with respect. Children learn respect or disrespect the same way they learn other values from us—by how we treat them and how they see us treat others.

Ironically, adults often try to teach children to be respectful by treating them disrespectfully. Many of us were taught disrespect by the words that were flung at us when we were children, and we sometimes hear those same damaging words coming out of our own mouths when our outrage overwhelms us.

Demanding respect from children just because we are their parents is a form of intimidation that will be effective only while they are small. Once they reach adolescence, many youth begin looking eye-to-eye with their parents—and not only in terms of physical stature. Many parents have discovered, when they can no longer demand respect because they are bigger and more threat-ening and therefore "deserve" it, just how little respect their teen-agers have for them. On the other hand, if we treat our children with respect, they will learn how to treat others—including their parents—with respect.

Erma Bombeck once wrote a hilarious parody of what it might be like if we talked to our friends the way we talk to our children. She starts by greeting her dinner party guests with, "Well, it's about time you two got here! What have you been doing? Dawdling?

Leave those shoes outside, Fred. They've got mud on them. And shut the door. Were you born in a barn?" She goes on to insist that her female guest wash her hands ("Don't tell me your hands are clean, I saw you playing with the dog") and that her male guest at least try the cauliflower or he won't be entitled to any dessert.

Needless to say, if we talked to our friends that way, they wouldn't continue to be our friends. However, our friends usually don't track muddy footprints through the house (for the millionth time) or leave wet, soggy towels on the bathroom floor (again!) or drop food on the floor because they weren't eating over their plates. And because our friends generally treat us with respect and dignity and seem to understand what "good" behavior is, we don't feel the need to treat them the way we often treat our children.

It may help to remember that children just don't think the same way we do. Perhaps they really don't remember they are supposed to hang up the wet towel. They may be so excited at the idea of arriving home that they run through the house with muddy shoes even though they've been told a million times not to. As annoying and frustrating as it may be, kids are often reckless, impulsive, and forgetful. We can give them gentle reminders that are respectful and compassionate, and someday, perhaps, they will learn these lessons along with the idea of how to be respectful to others.

Treating children with respect is sometimes a matter of changing our perceptions and vocabulary. Choose the words you use to describe your children carefully, particularly when addressing them or when they may overhear your conversation. For what a child hears, Doe says, becomes what she repeats about herself, and this will determine her self-worth and self-esteem. If we think a child is difficult, whiny, or frustrating, he is likely to pick up on this and develop a poor self-image. However, if we consider that same child as spirited, persistent, or assertive, we offer him a positive self-image that can mean a whole different direction in life.

Showing respect comes not only in the way that we talk to our children, but also in the way that we listen to them. Children know when we are giving them only cursory attention and are really more interested in the TV or the magazine we were reading. Yes, it can bore us to tears when we have to hear a detailed synopsis of the latest book for preteen girls or an enthusiastic description of the coolness of some action figure's conquest over evil. But these things are important to our children. If we don't at least act interested, they'll not only feel we don't care about what they have to say, they'll eventually stop sharing their ideas with us. This shutting down is most likely to happen during early adolescence, when we most want to keep those lines of communication open.

Accepting Children as They Are

The idea of respect involves not only understanding others, but accepting them as well. This is a hard bridge for most children to cross, and it's difficult for many adults as well.

Parents of special needs children are often told they need to let go of the dream of the child they imagined in order to appreciate the child they do have. All parents can use this advice. In order to truly affirm the uniqueness of our children, we must accept them just as they are, with all their challenges, frustrations, and idiosyncrasies. Only when we see children for who they really are, not who we wish they were, can we stop being disappointed that our son didn't make the team (even though he didn't really want to) or that our daughter doesn't want to become a doctor (she'd rather be a nurse, despite our attempts to educate her about how women no longer have to be limited to traditionally female-dominated occupations).

We also need to cushion our children against our uber-perfectionist culture, particularly in middle-class and more affluent school districts, where all too often, less than perfect equals failure. When the grading system was put in place in our schools, C meant "average"—the category that by definition, most children and youth would fall in. But in recent decades, C has taken on negative connotations, and anything less than a perfect A is considered substandard. Preparatory classes and special tutors have turned college entrance exams into a competitive sport, possibly out of the reach of many students. All the honor rolls, special awards, and honors classes push our children and adolescents to strive for success at all costs—often to the detriment of their own physical or mental health. But when we offer children acceptance for who they truly are, they are better able to withstand the pressures of the academic sphere.

This focus on high achievement for middle- and upper-class students not only results in an inordinate amount of stress, it also serves to further divide those students who have easy access to resources at home and at school from those children and youth who do not. Most Americans still believe that if a person works hard and studies, he or she can receive a quality education and be successful in life. However, in order for students to receive the best education in this country, they must have certain books in the home, access to the Internet and email, the willingness to sit still for long periods of time, and a familiarity with middle- and upper-class cultural references. For those who don't, merely obtaining a quality education can be an uphill battle, let alone scoring high on achievement tests or being selected for gifted education programs. And since children and youth spend so much time in school, the messages they receive about their capabilities and the expectations of them (high or low), can affect their self-esteem negatively. This low self-esteem often manifests itself through what is seen as traditionally "difficult" behavior such as acting out, losing assignments, or refusing to participate in groups.

It's not particularly easy to be accepting of our older children, especially when everything they say seems to be a direct criticism of us or when they engage in behavior that makes parenting challenging. It can be difficult to show teenagers the warmth and affection that may have come so easily when they were little, cute, and cuddly. In fact, the times when our older children and youth need our acceptance and love the most are, inevitably, those times when it is hardest to give it. Difficult behavior is often a cry for help, a plea that we as parents accept them—faults and all.

Modeling Radical Hospitality

We usually don't have to work at showing respect to people who are like-minded. It is much harder to show genuine respect for a person we don't agree with or even particularly like. However, truly accepting the inherent worth and dignity of all people means showing respect even toward those we disagree with. To this end, the idea of radical hospitality has been gaining popularity in many faith traditions, including Unitarian Universalism. As explained in the book *Radical Hospitality* by Fr. Daniel Homan and Lonni Gollins Pratt, the term means being open to "the other" who is different from us, and not only accepting those differences, but affirming them. Homan and Pratt write, "When we speak of hospitality we are always addressing issues of inclusion and exclusion. Each of us makes choices about who will and who will not be included in our lives." In this regard, hospitality takes on a moral dimension. When we decide who has the right to be included and who can be excluded, we are making judgments with moral implications.

Because we are human, we have a tendency to categorize people based on our prior experiences. This is how our brains work, but it also means we have a tendency to make assumptions about others. Assumptions are by their very nature often wrong, because they are conclusions reached without complete information. Assumptions can exclude people, result in unfair treatment, and perpetuate the systems of oppression still prevalent in our society today.

However, if we truly approach others with radical hospitality and the understanding that there is a divine spark within each person, we can offer everyone in our lives a loving kindness that goes beyond judgment or assumptions. The ability to look beyond differences and offer respect and kindness to others—even those we would not normally choose as our friends—can be a powerful tool of transformation. If we can model such behavior for our children, then they will learn that all people have inherent worth and dignity and deserve respect.

When we make it a habit to find and lift up the good in others, we can teach our children to let go of judgments and to find the spark within others that they can connect with. We show them how to recognize the rights and feelings of others and to use this recognition to guide their behavior. Modeling radical hospitality with the people we come into contact with offers the next generation a powerful guide for peaceful living.

As an adoptive and foster parent of special needs children, Liz Grimes has faced many challenges to her dedication to the first Principle. She says it can be very difficult to hold fast to the idea of inherent worth and dignity when a child or youth acts out in ways that are hurtful and sometimes seem intentional. However, sticking by her children even in the most difficult of times shows the other children in the family just how important it is to honor each person on their own journey. Grimes says that she and her husband tell every child who enters their home, "No one has to earn respect. No one is entitled to more respect than anyone else. The first and most important rule is respect for everyone. If you follow that, then everything else will follow and be rather easy."

Teaching Generosity

According to Berger, as children grow, they naturally become more generous toward others. Parents who insist that their children act generously before they are developmentally ready only delay this natural process. In fact, in the spirit of teaching children generosity, we often reinforce their feelings of selfishness. As adults, we are not required to hand over our grandmother's diamond ring to a houseguest, or give temporary possession of our prized autographed baseball to a friend who doesn't treasure it nearly as much as we do. Yet we regularly expect our children to share their favorite toys, lend their favorite books, or "play nice" when they see another child breaking the block tower they worked so hard to build. Insisting that children be generous under these circumstances only teaches them to dread the idea of sharing.

If your child is having friends over for a play date, talk to her before the guests arrive to determine what she is and is not willing to share. The toys she is willing to share can stay, but the most treasured items are best kept out of sight. If from time to time you box up toys that your child seems to have lost interest in, now might be a good time to get them out again. Once your child has agreed on what she will share, a reminder about your agreement during play time may be all that is needed.

You can also model generosity by letting your child witness your acts of kindness to others in need. Pay the toll for the person in the vehicle behind you, or ask your child to help you pick out cans of food for the food drive. Let your children see you giving money to the charities you support, and talk about why you support them. Let them stuff your dollar bills into the collection box.

Encourage children to give away some of their own money as well. Some parents invite their children to split any money earned into three separate jars: one for spending, one for saving, and one for giving. If your congregation doesn't have a separate children's offering, encourage your child to drop some of his own money into the plate or basket in the main service. Because each family is different, and financial giving is easier for some than others, you can encourage your child to place his contribution in a small envelope so that no one is aware of the amount given. And if your family budget does not allow for charitable giving, you can contribute your time, talents, and energies to causes you believe in and therefore model ways of giving beyond financial contributions. In fact, because the concept of money is pretty abstract for most young children, witnessing you giving in ways beyond writing out checks may actually make a greater impact on their future generosity.

As a present for birthdays or other occasions, instead of giving your child yet another toy that will soon be discarded, consider giving a certificate that promises you will donate a set amount of money to a charity of her choice. If she is not sure which charity to support, investigate some possibilities with her. For example, if she loves animals and is concerned about the environment, you could make a donation to help save an endangered species. Or consider sponsoring a child the same age as yours through organizations like Compassion International or World Vision. Writing letters to his sponsored "sibling" will have more impact on your child than trying to understand some vague notion of children starving on the other side of the world.

Generosity can also be demonstrated by giving family members coupons or certificates for services in lieu of purchased gifts or donations to charities. Children or adults can offer a coupon for "one free hug, good anytime" or a promise to take on an extra chore for a while.

Think about how you can involve your children in your volunteer opportunities in age-appropriate ways. Laura Yamashita took her young son, and later her daughter, with her to deliver meals to symptomatic AIDS patients, homebound seniors, and disabled adults. Parents, children, and youth can work together on many types of volunteer projects: serving meals in a soup kitchen, collecting for food drives, tending a community garden and donating the produce to a local homeless shelter, buying holiday gifts for a needy family, making greeting cards for nursing home residents. Talk about the values behind your actions: as your children pick out unwanted toys to donate to a domestic violence shelter, ask them how the children who receive them will feel.

As soon as they are able, encourage your children to write simple thank-you notes to express their appreciation for the gifts they receive. The exact words don't matter; just the act of writing the notes speaks to the intentionality of recognizing the kindness of others. After all, gratitude is the loving twin of generosity. When we feel grateful, we are often generous—and when we are feeling generous, it helps us be grateful.

Justice, Equity and Compassion

Children understand the basic concept of justice—being fair and doing what's right. However, depending on their moral and spiritual development, they may have a skewed perception of exactly what that means. For instance, preschoolers don't usually take a person's motivations into account; behavior is judged "good" or "bad" based on whether a reward or punishment will be received. Elementary-age children have a "law and order" mentality that emphasizes obeying rules without exception. During early adolescence, justice and injustice are perceived as polar opposites, with no gray area in between.

The challenge for parents, then, may be to stretch a child's idea of justice and fairness beyond his current stage of moral development. Focusing on the idea of equity rather than equality can be a way to communicate concepts of impartial justice. A discussion about equity causes us to ask what we are morally compelled to do in order to promote fairness.

So how do we teach our children, some of whom are growing up in relatively privileged homes, about the injustice of the world? How do we let them know that true justice goes beyond whose turn it is to choose a TV show and how bedtimes are determined?

For one thing, parents who regularly engage in social justice work can bring their children along and talk about what they are accomplishing with their actions. Participating in poverty reduction programs at your congregation, such as Guest at Your Table or Trick-or-Treat for UNICEF, can open the door to a conversation about poverty and injustice. Watching a movie or news program can prompt a discussion about what life is like for those facing racism, sexism, ageism, or other oppression.

Raising children in an anti-bias, anti-oppression home—one that acknowledges the realities of racism, the oppression of poverty, the danger of homophobia, and the error of making assumptions about ability—starts with the language we use and the environment we create in our home. We can teach our children to respect, appreciate, and affirm people who are different from them. We can actively work to not perpetuate harmful assumptions about others and help our own children to not internalize negative assumptions that are made about them. We can encourage our children to avoid teasing and name-calling and to stand up for themselves and others.

Appreciating Diversity

Parents can expose children of all ages to the concept of diversity and celebrate the gifts that diversity gives us. For example, you might hand a preschooler one crayon to color a whole picture with, then talk about the experience: "What would happen if the sky, the grass, the flowers, and the mountains were all the same color?"

You can use pretend play and storytelling to encourage children to grow their imaginations and take on new perspectives, says Sara Bullard in *Teaching Tolerance*. For instance, ask a child who lives in the suburbs to imagine what it might be like to live in a densely populated urban area or ask a child who lives in a large city what it might be like to live on a farm in the country. Where would she play? Who would be her friends? Where might she go to school? Investigate what it is like to live in different areas of the United States or in different countries of the world and invite your child to imagine growing up in the desert southwest; the great plains states; the New England area; or in Africa, Asia, or South America. How might life be different there? What language(s) might they speak? What kinds of foods might they eat? What would they do for fun?

To help your child appreciate cultural diversity, you can point out how many words in the English language actually originate from other cultures and languages. For example, your child may enjoy learning that words such as "rodeo" and "lasso" are actually Spanish words.

Exploring the idea of different gifts and talents can also teach children about diversity. While we can't all swim as well as Michael Phelps, who captured all those gold medals in the 2008 Summer Olympics, some of us can play a musical instrument beautifully or draw realistic pictures or write inspirational poetry. Reinforcing that we are all different, and that these differences make us special, promotes a sense of diversity.

Children and Stereotypes

While parents may dream of raising their children in a gender-free, race-neutral world where everyone is treated equally, in reality our society is far from this ideal. In addition, children are prone to stereotypical thinking at certain stages of their development.

Preschoolers do not necessarily understand that objects and people stay the same, even though their physical appearance may change. In this regard, their thinking is rather limited and inconsistent, which makes them susceptible to believing stereotypes. Since children's brains are wired to categorize new experiences in order to understand them, it is easy to see how they can arrive at conclusions that to us seem stereotypical. When a two-year-old sees another tall man in the grocery store and says "Daddy," we may think it is cute; but when he announces in public that a person of color looks like his day care provider, we may feel rather uncomfortable. It is up to us to help our children realize there are many different people in the world.

Once children reach the age of five or six, they are more group-oriented and can begin to understand the concept of cultural identity. They can also start to recognize stereotypes. However, children of this age are also very rule-oriented. Their continued need to categorize in order to understand the world can make for some rigid ideas about gender and racial behavior. Many Unitarian Universalist parents who have tried their best to raise gender-aware and gender-neutral children have been horrified when their son announces at the store, "Those toys are for girls—they're all pink," or when their five-year-old daughter announces matter-of-factly, "I can't play basketball. Basketball is for boys."

Playing games of categorizing can help to stretch a child's thinking. For example, you might show the child four toys—a red dinosaur, two blue dinosaurs, and a blue lizard—and ask which three are the same. If the child picks out the three blue toys, you can say, "That's right. Now can you find three others that are the same?" Help her see that three of the toys are dinosaurs, but only one is a lizard; or perhaps three are small and one is larger. Soon she will learn that the same four objects can be grouped in multiple ways, and she will begin to realize that categories are not fixed.

For another concrete example, remove the labels from several different cans of food. Ask children if they can tell what kind of food is inside just by looking at the can. Point out that although the cans look similar on the outside, they might be different on the inside. Then open the cans and let the children discover what is inside, and perhaps eat the food for lunch or dinner.

By age seven, children begin to understand that their physical appearance—hair, skin color, gender—will generally remain the same as they grow into adulthood. They also understand that cultural identity comes from family heritage. Children this age will pick up prejudices and stereotypes about themselves and others through their immature attempts to make sense of their world. Real-life encounters with diversity can activate children's subconscious stereotypes and trigger the related emotions without your even being aware of it. Unless you intervene, these stereotypes may not change.

Evaluate the toys, books, and TV programs that enter your home to determine what messages are sent. Do they present diverse images of people? Do they communicate the idea that we are all special because of these differences? Do they serve to break down stereotypes and negative images that oppress marginalized groups, or do they perpetuate them?

When they encounter persons with visible disabilities, young children may feel no hesitation in asking questions or commenting on bodily differences. This lack of self-censure can be uncomfortable for parents, but most children are merely curious and do not intentionally wish to offend. Their curiosity may result from their own fears or concerns about their physical state or from merely trying to understand the world and the nature of people. It's best to answer the child's questions in a way that is truthful and matter-of-fact, yet sensitive to the other person's feelings.

Although shushing a child who makes an inappropriate remark is often instinctive for humiliated parents, this only serves to send the message that the topic is off-limits. To be effective, conversations about race, ethnicity, disabilities, and gender stereotypes need to be explicit and concrete.

When you notice stereotypical images in television programs, videos, books, and magazines, point out that they are stereotypes and don't reflect reality. For instance, you can explain that although Native Americans might sometimes wear feathers, most Native American children wear ordinary clothes during everyday activities.

Some words and expressions perpetuate oppression by communicating negative messages, either explicitly or implicitly. For instance, phrases with the word *black*—*black sheep*, *black magic*, *black market*—generally have negative connotations, while phrases like *white knight* have positive meanings. Even coming out of the darkness into the light implies moving from ignorance to a state of knowing. When we pay attention to terms such as *Indian giver*, *white trash*, or *yellow-bellied*, we discover the power of words to communicate respect or, in these cases, disrespect and oppression.

Families of color know the power of words all too well. Recently one Unitarian Universalist parent, Catie Chi, confronted this issue head on when she took her son to a doctor's appointment. As they returned from the bathroom, they heard another child singing a derogatory song. Catie confronted the child with grace and dignity, explaining that this was not the place for such remarks. The boy's mother responded with a shrug and an offhand "I'm trying." Afterward, in their car, Catie was surprised to hear her son say that there were people like that everywhere and that we should be sad for them and grateful that we are not them. Hearing his words helped Catie heal her own anger and filled her with joy to realize what a big-hearted, compassionate person her son is.

Compassion

Although compassion is one of the most important values we can nurture in our children, our society continues to promote selfishness. This may make our job as parents more difficult, but not impossible. For example, highly competitive sports and rigorous academic programs that promote perfection can work against a child's development of compassion for others. Finding coaches who stress team-playing rather than winning, and promoting activities in which cooperation is stressed over competition, can go a long way toward helping children and youth break out of their natural egotistic tendencies.

As with most values, compassion is probably best taught in the home, by example. Expressing love and affection to your children shows them you care deeply about them. Listening respectfully when your child expresses feelings and thoughts also models compassionate behavior.

Children and youth also need to understand that being compassionate can help them create a better world. Developing a family tradition of community service, such as engaging in social justice projects together, communicates that compassion is a family value. Even the act of praying together for the well-being of others can go a long way toward nurturing compassion in our children and youth.

The selective use of stories, videos, and music can also promote a sense of compassion. Children who are regularly exposed to stories (real or fictional) of individuals behaving in compassionate ways toward one another receive powerful lessons on treating others well. After reading stories or viewing a program, take some time to talk about what happened and why the book or video emphasized the values you hope to promote. Ask your children what they think it must have felt like to be a particular character in the story. Doing so forces them to stretch their thinking and promotes critical analysis that can lead to their developing empathy for others.

Role playing can be an effective way of promoting justice through compassion. Asking children to act out a story or particular situation can help them come to an understanding of others' thoughts and feelings that is just not possible otherwise. This method turns the game of imagination into an active tool for learning about justice and compassion.

Speaking Out

Unitarian Universalist youth who grow up with an understanding of the inherent worth and dignity of all people and a commitment to justice, equity, and compassion are deeply offended when confronted with jokes, comments, or policies that perpetuate the oppression of marginalized people. However, they may need some help to channel their outrage in positive ways.

Since people often tell offensive jokes as a way of including some people by excluding others, adolescents who speak out about injustice may in effect be telling their friends that they do not want to be part of their group. This can be intimidating to the youth who wants to speak up, and can make the offending youth to feel defensive and lash out. However, simply doing nothing or ignoring the joke signifies approval. Refusing to hear oppressive or offensive remarks is a powerful tool for changing behavior.

Using "I" statements can help to defuse the situation and reduce the chance that the person telling the joke will react defensively. Saying something like "That joke makes me feel uncomfortable" is more likely to be effective than exclaiming, "That's racist!" Stating that the joke offends you personally carries more power than saying it might offend someone else. Youth who speak up may discover that other teens will thank them because they felt offended too, but were unsure what to say or do about it.

Shelter or Teach?

Some parents are concerned about how much ugliness in life children should be exposed to and at what ages, especially those with the resources to provide their children with sheltered lifestyles. Exposing our children to extreme poverty, suffering, addiction, or mental illness can be troublesome. But often when parents are concerned about such issues, it is because they are perceiving them from an adult perspective, not that of a child. When children help serve food at a soup kitchen, they learn that no one should go hungry. When children gather baby items for a home for unwed teenage mothers, they learn that even when people make poor choices, they deserve care, respect, and help to improve their lives.

Pain and suffering are part of life. Like the father of Siddhartha Gautama, the man who became the Buddha, we can shelter our children only for so long before they discover some of the ugliness in life for themselves. When we expose them to portions of it and communicate how we can all be a part of the solution, we teach our children about the true meaning of justice and compassion. The more they are able to contribute to solving the very real problems in our society, the more they will learn about themselves, and the more compassion they will have for others.

Likewise, when it comes to teaching our children about justice, equity, and compassion, we need to remember not to be silent or to assume that our children don't or won't understand. A recent study on children and prejudice revealed that when parents do not make an effort to address oppression and bias, they may unintentionally perpetuate them. If parents don't talk about issues of prejudice, justice, or diversity, children will absorb the attitudes of others around them or develop their own ideas, which then go unchallenged. Once again, parents are confronted with the reality that we cannot teach our children to have open minds when we close the door on the discussion—no matter how uncomfortable we may find that conversation to be.

Spiritual Growth
in Our Congregations

Many parents today, although feeling overwhelmed and stressed, are also spiritually hungry. We have a real need to find a sense of meaning in our lives. We also want to give our children the stable family that so many of us did not have, due to divorce and high mobility. However, many of us are raising our children far away from our own families of origin and extended support systems.

Our congregations can serve as the extended family and support system so many of our young families need. Yet many parents feel they are too busy to fit religious activities into their schedules. For children and youth, weekends and evenings are often taken up with extracurricular activities or jobs. While these activities can enrich the lives of our children, or may be necessary, they do little to strengthen the family as a whole and often serve to create divisions between family members.

Some parents may feel they don't need church because their theological beliefs are so different from what seem to be main-stream beliefs. They may feel they don't need to go to church in order to please a benevolent deity. Perhaps they prefer finding their spiritual moments in nature or through private rituals. Still, something often seems to be missing in the life of their family—a beloved community of like-minded individuals who welcome and support one another in both trying times and good times. All of us, but especially parents who are raising their children as freethinkers and spiritual seekers, need the support and encouragement that a beloved community offers.

Sometimes there is a Unitarian Universalist congregation nearby that fits the bill theologically, but includes few parents of young children or doesn't provide much support for parents and families. As Nancy Fuchs shares in *Our Share of Night, Our Share of Morning*, "There is nothing lonelier than being with people who are a community for each other but not for you." If you find yourself in this situation, perhaps there is another Unitarian Universalist congregation in your area that would be a better fit for your needs. If not, then it may be up to you to get involved in making your local congregation one that you can feel comfortable in. Healthy congregations—Unitarian Universalist congregations in particular —are not determined by effective professional leadership alone. It is the active involvement of parishioners that makes them the special places that they are.

A Community of Shared Values

A religious community helps us reinforce the values we want to teach our children. Values are perceived as more important if they are backed up by a group, particularly one with a strong tradition behind it. There is also a sense of comfort and security that comes from belonging to a group with shared core values. Rather than having to justify our values, we feel affirmed in our choices. We have the assurance of being part of something larger than ourselves—a tradition that was striving for those shared values before we were born and will continue after we die. We feel strengthened in our resolve should we meet resistance to our values and beliefs elsewhere.

Likewise, families that do not fit the traditional two-parent (one man, one woman) model are accepted and affirmed in Unitarian Universalist congregations. Here the phrase "family values" means that all families whose members love and strengthen one another have value.

Unitarian Universalist congregations highly value the individual search for meaning and recognize that truth has many forms. They not only offer support and acceptance of our religious beliefs, but also challenge us to consider those beliefs. Congregations have a myriad of learning opportunities available, from adult faith development classes to book study groups and special workshops. By being a part of a learning community that encourages curiosity and invites an ongoing quest for deeper understanding, we offer both our children and ourselves an atmosphere in which to thrive and develop in faith and spirituality.

Unitarian Universalist religious communities provide a diversity of people with different ideas, longings, backgrounds, and personalities. Simply by interacting with those different from ourselves, we learn something about the varieties of human nature. We get the chance to practice our values of respect, caring, and peace. And despite the diversity of theological beliefs and personal identities, we recognize that we all share common values defined by our Principles.

Many families will turn to a religious community during times of crisis or life transitions—when a family member dies, a baby is born, or a family is joined together in marriage or civil union. But our religious communities can and should be available to families even in the ordinary ups and downs of life. Within our beloved communities, we feel comfortable sharing our thoughts and feelings. We expect our fellow travelers to support us when we struggle through hard times and celebrate with us during the good times. This is the very essence of a beloved community.

Within such a community, our children can feel acceptance and affirmation of who they are and what they believe. For some children and youth, a Unitarian Universalist congregation may be the only place where this is the case. Nonbelievers in particular face a world full of prejudice and isolation, as do people who identify as bisexual, gay, lesbian, transgender, or questioning. Here they can be themselves without parsing their words and choosing their battles. In our congregations, youth don't have to worry about oppression because of their nonconformist ideas, and they receive support in their idealistic desire to change our wider world through social justice.

Children need religious education classes to learn about the Buddha's Middle Way, Martin Luther King Jr.'s approach to nonviolent social change, and Dorothea Dix's tireless campaign for social justice for the mentally ill. Children need to understand the importance of justice in our world and hear the great wisdom stories that offer timeless lessons about life. They also need to express their innate spiritual natures through joyfully singing songs of celebration, expressing heartfelt gratitude through prayers, or calming themselves through meditation. They need to hear stories that speak to their understanding and to internalize the rituals which make their religion unique. For these experiences, they need to participate in the very heart of the religious community, which is worship.

When They Don't Want to Go to Church

Sometimes it's not the parents, but children and youth who balk at taking the time to attend church. If you encounter resistance, try to determine the reasons behind it.

Despite the fact that a lot of time, effort, and expense goes into planning religious education classes, every child is an individual and has a particular learning style that may not be met by the RE program offered for his age group. In this case, it might be useful to talk to the religious educator or minister about the class your child attends and why he doesn't think it meets his needs. It may be that this feedback is just what is needed to improve the program, or together you may be able to find another creative alternative way to involve your child in the life of the congregation.

However, once children reach elementary school age, the main reason they balk at attending church has nothing to do with curricula or programming. It is because they feel they have not made any friends or do not feel comfortable with the group. Community building and mixer activities are essential for elementary-age children, as well as purely social activities that bond the group together. If your congregation does not offer these activities or emphasize community building, talk to your religious educator. If necessary, volunteer to organize an activity to bring the children together as a cohesive group and build friendships.

No matter why your elementary-age child doesn't want to attend church, the most important thing you can do is to not give in. Many children will resist going to church (and participating in other activities) in order to test you and to establish their autonomy within the family. You can simply present attending services and religious education classes as nonnegotiable, just like brushing teeth, going to school, or wearing a seat belt. You might inform your child in a matter-of-fact manner, "This is what we do on Sundays." Treat family church attendance as a priority and a commitment that is just as important as involvement in scouting, band, or sports teams. Your child will resist less over time when she understands that you will remain consistent on this issue. As parent and religious educator Annie Scott says, "We made our children go to church because we valued their spirituality and our family's belonging to a Unitarian Universalist covenantal community. It didn't make the issue magically disappear, but our decisions and insistence were based on the values we held for our family."

If you communicate that church is an important priority for your family, then you need to show your children that this goes for you as well as for them. Model the desired behavior by attending church every Sunday rather than choosing to stay home when you're tired or need to paint the house. If one parent does not attend with the rest of the family (because of differing beliefs, for example), you can explain to your child why the adult has made the choice to stay home and that there is a difference between the decisions that adults and children are permitted to make.

If you're concerned that "forcing" elementary-age or younger children to attend church goes against our value of freedom of belief, it may help to know that resistance to attending church is often nothing more than resistance to leaving the house. Many children who appear to protest week after week actually enjoy themselves once they arrive at church. However, if you want to give your children a choice, you might suggest that they choose whether to go to their religious education classes, stay in the worship service with you, or find some other way to be a part of the religious community.

The religious educator or the minister may be able to suggest alternatives, such as helping out in the nursery or the kitchen.

As parent Lynn Gunney explains, "If we truly love and cherish our values as Unitarian Universalists, we must love them enough to insist that our kids experience the benefits of them throughout their development. Children are really in very different places in their understanding and outlook on the world at different stages in their lives, and if we don't bring them to church regularly as these stages come and go, they have missed the opportunity to examine these issues through the lens of the UU perspective."

When it comes to youth, the decision about whether to attend church becomes more complicated. Sometimes just getting teenagers to recognize that they have a spiritual side is tough enough; encouraging them to nurture that part of themselves is a real challenge. If they don't feel that church is meeting their needs (spiritual or otherwise), then they will actively resist attending. As many parents have discovered, requiring adolescents to participate in anything against their wishes can cause them to loathe the experience. Forcing teenagers to attend church can cause deep resentment toward not only their parents, but the religious community as well. Besides, one of our jobs as parents is to encourage our youth to learn to make their own decisions while they are still in a safe environment. If they are not allowed to make any decisions that we do not agree with, how will they ever become independent?

Usually, youth who do not want to attend church have the same reason as some adults: they don't feel there is anything of value there for them. If they don't feel connections with others, and if they aren't given opportunities to express their deeper selves and to do good in the world through social action, then they are not motivated to attend or participate in congregational activities.

In cases like this, try to discover what your teenager wants out of church, and then talk to the religious educator or minister about finding or creating those opportunities. If there is no youth group, perhaps one could be formed. If there aren't enough teens to form a youth group, perhaps your teen could help organize activities for younger children or join an adult social action project. Look for ways your youth might connect to your faith through district events or by organizing an activity with another congregation's youth group. If there are other nearby Unitarian Universalist congregations, check them out to see if they feel more welcoming to your youth.

It is an unfortunate reality that many of our congregations are considered boring, irrelevant, and out of touch with the needs of today's youth. It's no wonder that so many of our teens balk at attending. Youth grow weary of hearing a lot of negative statements about other religious traditions. They also have a strong "hypocrisy meter" that can easily detect inconsistencies, and they can become disappointed when it doesn't seem as if their religious home lives up to the ideals that they were taught to believe in.

Youth often receive mixed messages about their very presence in the faith community. When they were younger, the congregation may have lifted them up as both cute and profound. But when they reach their teens and twenties, they are often ignored or even put down. Chris Hackett, author of the online article "Why Don't Young People Come to Church?" explains, "The older generation doesn't take us seriously. We are told by the older generation to get involved in church. When we do, we are told to come on Sunday mornings, and leave mission work and money issues for the older generation to handle." Until we can learn to affirm our youth and embrace them wholeheartedly into our religious communities, many young people will go elsewhere to find a place for their spiritual expression.

The Search for Truth and Meaning

Our fourth Unitarian Universalist Principle can be both a blessing and a challenge to overcome. Time and again, when asked to identify the most difficult part of raising children in our faith, parents of all backgrounds and life circumstances respond with some variation on the theme of not having any set answers, creed, or certainty to give their children. However, many of these same parents also say that one of the greatest joys of raising children as Unitarian Universalists was helping them to become freethinking and open-minded people.

For example, Christine Prado says that "the questions are harder to answer because the church doesn't give us pat answers." And yet, one of the best things about parenting her Unitarian Universalist children was that "they have to think harder about the tough questions." Likewise, Sheri Phillabuam says the challenges and blessings of raising children in our faith are inseparable. "With no central charismatic figure or simple, easy-to-grasp creed," she says, "it's difficult to help young children define themselves religiously." But since children are challenged to think for themselves, our faith "allows for an unlimited exploration of what it means to be human and live in the world."

The Questioning Spirit

At the heart of our religious tradition is the idea of questioning, seeking, wondering, exploring, and even changing our minds when new things become important. Children, in particular, have a natural curiosity about the world and about life. One of their most frequent questions is "Why?" Unitarian Universalist children are not likely to simply take an adult's answer at face value. There are always more questions. Often the adults who are being queried can become flustered by the follow-ups, particularly when they believe they did a good job of articulating a thoughtful response in the first place.

Rather than quash that curiosity, we need to find ways to affirm and encourage it. Robert Kay, a psychiatrist and author, cautions parents never to criticize children for asking questions. However, he adds that this doesn't mean we can't groan if the question is badly timed or is inappropriate to a given situation.

Asking our own questions in the presence of our children is another powerful way to encourage their natural curiosity. Saying out loud, "I wonder why this tastes so salty" or "I wonder why I feel like dancing when I hear music" shows our children that asking questions is part of our human quest to understand the world.

The Gift of Not Answering

Although our children are hungry for answers, sometimes supplying them is the least helpful thing we can do. Depending on the question, it may be better to encourage children to try figuring out the answer on their own. Doing so strengthens their reasoning skills, boosts their confidence, and lets them experience the pleasure of discovery.

There are a variety of ways to encourage children to keep questioning without providing the answers for them. One option is to say something like, "That's a great question. What do you think the answer might be?" Then ask follow-up questions to help the child reach the true answer, or offer it after the child has made a guess. Be careful, however, not to say or imply that the child's answer is silly or immature. Remember that children often make what adults would consider illogical leaps in order to fill gaps in their understanding. Ridiculing incorrect answers closes the door to further questioning and discovery. Instead, you might initiate a conversation that helps the child realize why her answer can't be true.

Another approach is to respond to a child's question with a funny answer, one that is clearly not true. This not only injects some humor into the situation, but also encourages the child to formulate her own ideas, because she can readily see that your answer is not right.

A response of "I don't know," followed by "but let's find out together," serves the dual purpose of encouraging questions and helping children discover where to find answers. Introducing your child to the rich resources that are available (books, the Internet, documentary films, and so on) establishes both a lifelong appreciation for seeking answers and the tools and skills for finding them. Just as it is better to teach someone to fish than to hand out fish, showing your child how to look for his own answers is more powerful than merely supplying him with the answers.

Some questions have no answers. Fortunately, most children —even very young ones—are used to living with a certain amount of ambiguity. After all, their world is full of uncertainty. They learn about divorce and wonder whether their parents will stay together. They learn about death and are concerned about when they or their loved ones will die. Psychiatrist Robert Kay says that the answer "I don't know" is one of the greatest gifts a parent can give to a child's intellectual development. Acknowledging that something is beyond our grasp is powerful and affirming, because it allows a child to accept that some things are simply unknowable.

We can also help our children understand that different people have different ideas about some questions. We can explain that our ideas may change over time as we gain more information and more experience. Understanding how our thinking changes as we mature can help children feel less threatened when their own thinking begins to change. Unitarian Universalist religious educator Sophia Lyon Fahs suggested parents can respond with: "This is something grown-ups have been thinking about for a long time. We don't have the whole answer, but we have something we can say about it, and what you don't understand today, you may understand a little better when you're still older than you are now. Who knows, you may even come up with answers to it that no one has ever thought of before, as you continue to try to understand it."

Purpose and Meaning

Although children can accept that life is full of uncertainty, they also need to know that it has purpose. As Mimi Doe says in *10 Principles for Spiritual Parenting*, "Trusting that all life has a purpose gives our children meaning in a complex and confusing world. It grounds them when they feel tossed and battered by external events." Wherever it comes from—perhaps the belief that we are part of some grand plan created by a higher power, or the idea that we are connected with all of the universe—a sense of meaning helps children understand that what we do matters. Even if we believe that life is without inherent meaning, we face the challenge of creating our own purpose and teaching our children to do so as well.

Psychiatrists have suggested that pondering the meaning of life—and our own lives in particular—is good for our mental and emotional well-being. Since we are all unique individuals, it makes sense to believe that each of us finds meaning in our own individual ways. Perhaps our purpose in life is to explore what our special talents are and how we can best contribute to the universe, whether through involvement in a particular cause or simply following our personal passions.

By understanding and accepting our children's preferred ways to embrace life, we can offer soulful activities that help them to uncover their talents. Says Doe, "What gives a child joy may become her passion, and by pursuing her passion she will fulfill her soul's purpose. By filling her soul's purpose she will oftentimes be making the world a better place."

Opposing Points of View

Despite our best intentions to raise freethinking children who understand the possibilities for many different religious truths, we live in a world that often rejects such possibilities and, through ignorance or distrust, frowns on religious nonconformity. Even as our country grows more religiously diverse, the general populace remains intolerant of atheists, agnostics, and humanists. Since most people's notions of right and wrong are inextricably tied to their religious beliefs, they often assume that anyone who does not believe in a higher power has no sense of morality.

Pagans have also been painted in a negative light, in part because of the historical conflict between dominant religious cultures—with their view of a male, patriarchal, monotheistic God—and Goddess-centered religions that adhere to a feminine image of the divine. Wiccans, in particular, have been associated with devil worship by uninformed people who assume the historical allegations of such behavior to be literally true.

Even Unitarian Universalist families who consider themselves theists or Christians, often face rejection by people who have been taught that their own understanding is the only truth possible. Although more and more young people identify themselves as "spiritual" rather than "religious," the volume of right-wing evangelical rhetoric in our culture often drowns out the voices of more moderate and progressive Christians or theists.

Because we as parents are often far removed from the angst of youth, it can be difficult for us to realize just how strongly our children want to fit in with their friends and how troubling it can be for them to express religious ideas that lie outside of the mainstream. Particularly during the "law and order" years of elementary school, it is hard for children to understand that one belief is not more or less true than another. In their world of extremes, where everything is either right or wrong, being part of a family with beliefs that are so different feels wrong. Being different also opens them up to potential harassment, bullying, and even violence—

especially if their peers think that nonbelievers are immoral or that being pagan is the equivalent of devil worship.

As Kristin Madden reveals in *Pagan Parenting*, "I learned at a very young age to keep my mouth shut about the alternative activities of my family, and I lived a double life for many, many years. Times have changed, but not so much that all pagan families can feel comfortable blatantly discussing our family's spirituality or metaphysical beliefs with just anyone. We don't want our children to be ashamed of our lifestyle, but we would be foolish not to recognize the need to be discreet."

As Madden points out, children do not have the options for escape that many adults do. Adults can maintain separate social groups of casual acquaintances and close friends, and if some relationships become troublesome, they may be able to move or change jobs. But children are more or less stuck with their peer group at school. Their choices are to be completely honest—thus risking rejection, betrayal, and proselytizing by friends determined to save their souls—or, more likely, to pretend to conform. It is up to each youth to determine the best decision, and that decision may change depending on the circumstances.

As parents, we can sometimes feel overwhelmed with the need to protect our children, particularly if they are facing bullying or teasing. But if we become overly protective, we prevent our children from dealing with real life issues that they will have to face sooner or later. As Madden says, "The best way we can prepare our children is to talk to them about all the possibilities," just as we discuss the possible consequences of unprotected sex or the dangers of drug abuse.

When most of their peers belong to a different religion, children and youth are likely to feel alienated and isolated. They may begin to resent their parents and perhaps even accuse them of causing them difficulties. Participation in a Unitarian Universalist youth group, or contact with other youths who are open to religious diversity, can make a big difference in combating that sense of isolation. Being part of a youth group also affirms an adolescent's emerging sense of identity and cements the value of being a unique individual.

We can stress to our children that although we live in a society that claims to appreciate diversity, it often falls far short of the ideal. It may be tempting to tell your teenager that true friends would accept her for who she is. But while she is hurting, she is focusing on the fact that the hurt was inflicted in the name of her religious beliefs. If she is not discouraged from thinking that her unorthodox beliefs are the problem, she may end up rejecting those beliefs. Help her to understand that the fault lies not in her beliefs, but in the narrow views of her friends. Remind her that we do not have to agree with people in order to respect them and honor their inherent worth and dignity, but not all religious traditions preach the same message. Although Jesus taught love of one's neighbors, this kind of acceptance does not always happen in practice. Sometimes people are not even aware that alternative viewpoints are possible; they may have been so indoctrinated in their faith that they were never exposed to the possibility of different beliefs.

We can also communicate to our children and youth that in our view, the purpose of religion is not to establish absolute truths; that is the role of science. Religious beliefs are concerned with truths, but should be considered more of a vehicle for arriving at a truth rather than the only destination possible. Since faith—unlike science—does not require provable facts or tested theories, the nature of belief is more subjective than objective. Not only is faith personal and individual, beliefs about life and the world may even change over our lifetimes. Scientific beliefs, on the other hand, are only altered when overwhelming evidence points to faulty studies or new information which opens up a new way of thinking.

It takes great courage to stand up for one's beliefs, particularly if youth fear they are alone in their ideas. However, a youth may discover a strong sense of affirmation when he reveals his religious beliefs and finds them validated by his friends. He may even find that his friends think similar thoughts and may be interested in learning more about what it means to be a Unitarian Universalist. Eventually, perhaps, your youth will understand that true friends do respect the beliefs of others, even if they don't agree with them, and that it is okay—in fact, it is wonderful—to be unique and different.

Sources of Truth

Many religions have one or more sacred texts that are a source of truth for their faith, often inspired by or considered to be the very word of the Divine. However, Unitarian Universalism has no one book, or even a series of books, that contains all of our truths. In fact, talking to any two people at the same Unitarian Universalist congregation will probably yield not only two different religious philosophies, but also two different ideas of where to look for answers. We believe the search for truth is an individual one, and although it may be conducted within a community of like-minded souls, what is meaningful and relevant for one person may not be so for someone else.

Unitarian Universalism has sometimes been characterized (often by misinformed youth) as a religion where "we can believe anything we want." This statement is not really accurate, because it implies we can make up whatever we want to believe. In reality, Unitarian Universalists engage in a lifelong search for truth and meaning. While our views and ideas may change over the years, this quest for understanding through study and reflection is taken quite seriously.

Although we believe religious authority lies within each individual, as a group, we draw inspiration from the teachings, practices, and wisdom of the world's religions and other philosophies, including humanism, earth-centered spiritual traditions, mysticism, theism, skepticism, naturalism, process thought, and feminist and liberation theologies. These myriad sources of authority can be likened to a buffet where we choose the options that are most palatable to our tastes and most compatible with the items already on our plates.

We recognize the importance and power of direct experiences of mystery and wonder, beauty and joy, and creative and artistic expression. At the same time, we look to the guidance of reason, rationality, logic, and science to inform our thinking. More and more Unitarian Universalist parents are discovering that to be truly and fully informed, we must use both the creative, feeling parts of our brains and the thinking, rational parts of our brains. Since so much of life is inherently unknowable in a rational sense, intuition and emotion must also play a big role in our belief formation and our quest for understanding.

This dichotomy is not as troubling for children as it can be for some adults. Since children by nature are more intuitive and sensitive to their emotional states (even if they are unable to articulate or act on this awareness), then it follows that children don't need to be taught how to appreciate and learn from wonder. Instead, we as parents need to find ways to nurture their innate sense of spirituality. Through encouraging and affirming our children's sense of natural curiosity about the world, it is possible to rekindle the spark of wonder in our own lives that may have been lost over the years. When understanding is ultimately beyond our grasp and rational answers elude us, it may be necessary to take a leap of faith—to rely on our intuition and creative insights.

The Right of Conscience

We do not raise our children in a bubble, and the world in which they are coming of age is far from ideal. Although we do our best to instill our personal values through modeling and teaching, our children have to interact with others in a world of intolerance, discrimination, hatred, and oppression. We teach our children about the inherent worth and dignity of all persons, yet they confront bullies in their schools who get a charge out of putting others down. We appreciate their questioning minds and excite their curiosity, then see their frustration with rote learning and memorization of facts in schools. And we encourage them to stand on the side of justice, equity, and compassion, even as they witness their friend of color or experience themselves continually being passed over in class while knowing the answer to the teacher's question.

When we think of the fifth Principle, we tend to focus on the words "the use of the democratic process within our congregations and in our society at large" and gloss over what is arguably the most important part—"the right of conscience." When it comes to raising children as Unitarian Universalists, this phrase takes on great significance. Knowing when to speak up and stand up for justice is a challenge faced by our children and youth on an almost daily basis. They feel compelled to act; after all, these are the values we sought to instill in them. But confronting opposition and oppressive ideas in the wider world is not easy.

Critical Thinking

Unitarian Universalism encourages children and youth not only to seek answers to their questions, but to question authority. When we teach them to "consider the source" when making decisions and formulating their religious beliefs, we are in essence teaching them critical thinking skills. Critical thinking and questioning authority are not always compatible with public schools and other institutions. Nevertheless, they are the key to progress itself. Many of the most important moments in history can be attributed to people who had the integrity to question authority. Affirming our children's ability to think for themselves is a tremendous gift not only to them, but to the world.

All difficult choices force us to examine our true beliefs and follow the counsel of our conscience. As Mimi Doe informs us in *10 Principles for Spiritual Parenting*, the very act of connecting with our value system leads to creative solutions to the problems we face. If your child is having trouble making a specific decision, Doe suggests you "ask him to step back from the dilemma and ask himself questions like: What is the right thing to do in this situation, according to who I am and what I believe in?"

Taking a Stand

Although doing what is consistent with your values feels right, it is not always easy to stand on the side of justice when it seems you are standing alone. We can support and encourage our children and youth to stand up for what they believe in, but when push comes to shove, they will be the ones risking friendships, ostracism, and ridicule. This is why once children reach the preteen years, we must take their feelings and concerns into account before taking any stand on their behalf. We can encourage them to take healthy risks and push past their comfort zone, but in the end, they are the ones venturing out on a limb. We must be ready to help them feel successful and supported should that limb wobble or even break.

When Stu Tanquist's daughter brought home a "values assessment" from her public school health class, he was incensed. The assessments were clearly skewed to show that nonbelievers were subject to more stress, lower moral values, and more depression and other sources of mental illness. Despite his immediate reaction, Stu first consulted his daughter over whether she had concerns about his pursuing the matter. She told him that she, too, was insulted and that she would like him to do something about it. Through the entire process, she remained proud that her family had the courage to do the right thing.

Unitarian Universalist children and youth who decide to opt out of prayers spoken by a team member in the locker room, or who refuse to recite the Pledge of Allegiance because it includes the phrase "under God," risk ostracism and ridicule. However, because they are the ones who will need to stand in the line of fire, ultimately it needs to be their decision. If you and your child decide to pursue such an issue, never lose sight of the goals—not only resolving the issue in the interests of your child but, whenever possible, bringing about lasting change. Darwin Bromley, a Unitarian Universalist from Florida, was shocked when his sixth grader came home from public school with a final exam that included the extra credit question, "Who is your savior?" His daughter was as outraged as he was, and they pursued the issue. Today the teacher who gave the exam is no longer employed at that school.

The Case of the Boy Scouts

Parents have discovered that challenges to other institutions can be much more difficult. An atheist parent, Margaret Downey describes the ordeal she and her son went through after moving to Illinois from New Jersey. Since her son had been active in the Boy Scouts in their previous community, they found another troop in their new home. However, when the new troop leader looked through the handbook of Downey's son and noticed a page where the word *God* was replaced with *good*, the leader thundered, "What are you—

some kind of *atheist?*" The leader's tone of voice and manner so upset the boy that he broke into tears when he returned home. He told his mother that they needed to find a religion or he would not be allowed to return to a scout meeting.

Because the troop in New Jersey had been so accepting of their nonbelieving stance, Downey at first assumed the reaction was just a peculiarity of the one troop and an overzealous leader, so when they moved to Pennsylvania, her son again tried to get involved in the Boy Scouts. However, after sending in his application with the word *God* crossed out and replaced with *good*, she was surprised to receive a letter from the national headquarters with a rejection and the official statement that "no boy can grow into the best sort of citizen without recognizing an obligation to God." Downey felt demeaned, as if her family's patriotism was in question and their ethics of honesty, kindness, and courage were challenged. She filed a complaint of discrimination against the Boy Scouts of America (BSA) in 1991.

It took the Pennsylvania Human Rights commission nine years to investigate Downey's complaint, and when the details of the case were disclosed, her whole family suffered. They received death threats, her husband's job was in jeopardy, and one week before Downey's son was to graduate from high school, his name was leaked to the press. After all this, the Downey family eventually lost the case. In 2001, the BSA declared itself a private organization, no longer serving the community at large, which gave it the right to discriminate against whomever it chose. Not long afterward, the BSA announced that it would no longer award Unitarian Universalist scouts the Religion and Life award, because the denomination was considered too accepting of gay people and atheists.

Since then, many Boy Scout troops across the United States have been disbanded by the national office for protesting the national membership policy that excludes atheists and gay people. The Boy Scout organization has also lost funding from public institutions like the United Way, which withdrew its financial support because of the private institution designation. Despite all this, the BSA remains steadfast in its right to discriminate. Now each Unitarian Universalist family must decide for themselves whether to participate in an organization that, while offering many potential benefits, promotes intolerance.

Jan Devor describes how her family dealt with this dilemma: "We were faced with this decision in our own family when our son asked to join the Boy Scouts in early elementary school. At that time, we simply said that we disagreed with a number of positions that the BSA takes as a group and thus he wouldn't be joining. In the later elementary years, we talked to our son about the specific policies that we believed were ethically wrong."

On the other hand, one Unitarian Universalist parent from Massachusetts believes that the merits of her son's participation in Boy Scouts outweighs any objection she has to the national organization's policies. While she doesn't approve of the BSA's objection to gay leaders or the insistence that scouts profess a belief in God, she also thinks that her children have to learn to cope in a world that has different views. She considers it simply good practice for life, and she will encourage her sons to engage with those they disagree with in a loving way and help to educate them through this engagement.

Offering Support

There will be times when we are called to stand by and watch as our children and youth follow their conscience and fight their own battles with the system. While it is not easy, we must allow them that opportunity to grow and shine. We also need to offer them our support and loving guidance. We need to help our youth identify their concerns and express them in an assertive, yet respectful manner. We must encourage them to stand up for what they think is the right thing to do, even when it seems as if they are outnumbered or intimidated by those who insist on submission and obedience.

Cara Cook, who grew up in northern Indiana, stood by her belief that using stereotypical Native American images and slogans to motivate her school to defeat another team in the homecoming game was wrong. She pursued her convictions to the principal's office on multiple occasions. The resulting backlash was a social nightmare. Cara eventually decided to drop out of school and obtain a GED rather than receive a diploma from the institution that she fought against. Despite their concerns, her parents supported her. They recognized that in this fight, she was embodying the values they had taught her when they raised her to believe in herself and her right of conscience. Cara went on to receive a bachelor's degree from a prestigious university and continues her social justice activism today.

Peace, Liberty and Justice for All

Many people have the mistaken impression that to have peace, we must be free of conflict. However, conflict is an inevitable part of life and leads to growth opportunities. The key, then, is to teach our children how to engage positively with conflict and interact constructively with others—even with those with whom they disagree.

The family can serve as a laboratory in which children learn how to solve conflicts peacefully, forgive siblings when feelings are hurt, express honest feelings with caring words, and truly listen to one another. In the home, with their siblings and parents, children and youth can learn important skills for peacemaking in the world.

Nonviolent Communication

The process known as nonviolent communication (NVC) was developed by Marshall Rosenberg to encourage compassionate understanding. It is a way of relating to ourselves and others by honestly expressing our personal needs and empathizing with the needs of others. Practitioners of NVC avoid making judgments or offering criticisms, which so often lead to defensive and hostile responses. When we learn to identify our needs, express them clearly, and listen actively to the needs of others, we can practice peaceful interactions despite the presence of conflict.

In his book *Nonviolent Communication*, Rosenberg writes that when NVC is practiced, "instead of being habitual, automatic reactions, our words become conscious responses based firmly on an awareness of what we are perceiving, feeling, and wanting. We are led to express ourselves with honesty and clarity while simultaneously paying others a respectful and empathetic attention." Essentially, the goal of NVC is to find a way for all parties in the conflict to get what really matters to them without the use of guilt, humiliation, shame, blame, coercion, or threats. Given that these very tools are frequently what parents use to demand cooperation from their children, this may require a new mind-set.

The first step is to report observations without judgment or evaluation of any kind. This lack of evaluation is crucial, because directly observable facts provide a common ground for communication. For example, saying to a child "This room is a mess" makes a value judgment. It places the child in the position of either rejecting your evaluation (the room isn't messy) or defending the state of disarray in the room (it's okay for my room to be messy). Instead you could say, "I need the floor clear in your room so I can get to your closet without stepping on something." This statement does not express a judgment or criticism, but simply an observation (there are items on the floor) and a feeling or need (I must get to the closet).

Once you have made an observation and expressed a need, you can then make a concrete request for action to meet the need. However, to make this a real request and not just another demand, you must allow the other person to say "no" or propose an alternative suggestion. Saying, "I would appreciate it if you could take care of this problem after school tomorrow," opens the door to further discussion rather than a demand which can be rejected outright or done resentfully. However, this also allows your child to respond with an alternative suggestion, perhaps with a promise to clean up the room on Saturday since she is way too busy to do it on a weekday. Then a simple reminder of this promise should be all that is needed on the weekend: "Do you remember our conversation about your room and how I need to be able to get to your closet without worrying about stepping on anything?" Again, even the reminder is offered in the form of the parent's need with a subtle request of whether or not the child recalls the conversation.

Active Listening

When a child sees that her feelings are acknowledged and accepted, she will feel affirmed and will likely change her behavior as a result.

Suppose your child of six or seven declares, "I hate you." If you take offense and focus on the venom expressed in that sentiment, the conflict will only escalate, and no one will feel good about the outcome. Despite the anger in your child's voice, she does not truly hate you. More likely, she is angry about something you have done or said and is not able to articulate her real feelings.

Instead of responding with anger, use active listening. Mirror the child's words and name an emotion that could be behind them: "You hate me right now. You must be pretty angry." By mirroring the child's words, you acknowledge them as valid. By naming an emotion, you help the child understand what she is feeling. If the child is in fact angry, she will probably admit it at this point; if she is not, then she may be able to explain how she actually feels, such as sad. Either way, the situation has been somewhat defused and you can begin to address the heart of the issue.

In response to your active listening, the child is likely to make further statements about what is bothering her. For example, she might say, "You are so mean to me." Resist the temptation to respond with, "Of course I'm not mean to you! I treat you better than I should, and you take advantage of me at every turn." Such a response will probably cause her to clam up and become even more resentful. Instead, simply continue to mirror the child's words: "You feel I am mean to you." Keep the emphasis on the child's feelings, without judgment or correction. It is futile to argue with children about whether their feelings are "right"—feelings are feelings. How they act on those feelings may be up for debate, but the feelings themselves are never wrong.

Hopefully, your active listening will allow your child to calmly explain why she thinks you are mean. If, however, she is still having trouble articulating her feelings, you could try to describe the situation and ask for clarification: "You think I'm mean because I won't let you have a cookie right now. Is that it?" This approach allows the child to either acknowledge your observation as accurate or offer an alternative explanation. It also continues to validate her feelings without necessarily condoning her behavior.

When a conflict arises, active listening is best used early in the process, particularly in the case of younger children. Once a child has become overrun with emotions and is kicking, screaming, or flailing about, nothing productive will happen until you are able to calm the child down. In the case of a meltdown, consider whether the child is too hungry, tired, or overstimulated to participate in the activity at hand. Perhaps a healthy snack or a change of environment is all that is needed to defuse the situation.

Sibling Rivalry

It's hard to say who is more irritated by the daily battles between siblings: the children or the parents. The subjects of these disputes may seem absurd and petty to adults, but they are rarely the real issues. Control, power, and self-worth are usually at the heart of these skirmishes. Winning these battles becomes a matter of proving who is more worthy, lovable, or appreciated and taps into the deepest part of a child's self-esteem and doubt. As Isabelle Fox describes in her book *Growing Up*, "Children don't know how to ask for a smile, a hug or a cheerful and heartfelt word of appreciation, but they do know how to fight and bicker over what is tangible in their world."

To understand sibling rivalry, it may help to recognize the dynamics of birth order. Oldest children have a tendency toward perfectionism and are very hard on themselves when they don't perform as well as they feel they should have. They generally feel more stress and anxiety about taking new steps and entering into new life stages. Younger children, on the other hand, are more likely to struggle with confidence issues, because they want to be like their older siblings but feel less competent. They may feel that they will never really be able to measure up to their more capable older siblings.

Older and younger siblings also differ in how they instigate conflict. Older siblings often feel resentful at what they perceive to be preferential treatment of the younger child. Younger children can become quite skilled at provoking angry responses in their older siblings, who then get in trouble for lashing out at the younger, supposedly more defenseless child.

In addition to understanding the influence of their children's birth order, it is helpful for parents to recognize the influence of their own position in their family of origin. You may unconsciously show favoritism toward the child who occupies the same position in the family that you did when you were growing up, because you can empathize with the challenges of that role. On the other hand, you may hold that child to a higher standard, believing that he should "tough it out" just like you had to. Even parents who have no siblings may approach sibling rivalry with their own bias, feeling frustration when their children seem not to appreciate their brothers and sisters. Parents who were the middle children of their families are likely to approach their children's sibling rivalry the most realistically, because they know what it is like to be both an older sibling and a younger one.

Conflict Resolution

Whether conflicts stem from sibling rivalry or playground squabbles with friends, there is genuine value in helping children learn how to resolve their own differences. But children first need the skills to do so. Until they learn positive ways of managing conflict, parental intervention may be necessary. This is especially true for sibling conflicts, given that older children are generally stronger, more intimidating, and more skilled verbally than their younger siblings.

Children can be taught to use nonviolent communication and active listening to address conflicts with their friends and siblings.

The process will be easier if your children have seen you model these techniques. You will probably need to coach them in how to clarify their feelings, express their needs, and offer observations without judgment. Although children tend to be more emotional and intuitive than adults, they also have less ability to name their emotions and to recognize when they are acting on feelings of anger or sadness.

Consider using a specific symbol or word to acknowledge conflict and start the resolution process. Linda Rice, a preschool teacher at a Montessori school, uses a "peace rose." When two children are in conflict in her classroom, either child can ask for the rose, or Rice may tell the children that she believes they need to go get the peace rose. This action calls a halt to what is going on and signals the children that the conflict needs to be resolved.

Having the peace rose as a tangible symbol helps the children remember what they are to do. The child who is holding the peace rose gets to talk while the other person listens and reflects words and feelings back. Then the other child holds the rose and gets a chance to speak. An adult may need to remind both children to stick to expressing their own feelings and thoughts, rather than making judgments about the other person.

Another approach might be to have each child role-play the other person's point of view. Putting themselves in the other person's shoes and explaining why they acted as they did can help increase empathy and understanding.

Any object can be used in place of the peace rose, as long as it does not belong to either of the children involved and is set aside specifically for this purpose. The first few times this, or any, technique is used, the process may not go smoothly. But with patience and continued effort, the ritual will become clear. Eventually the mere presence of the peace object will alter behavior and move both parties toward resolution. You may even find your child telling you and your spouse or partner to get the peace rose when you have a conflict.

Forgiveness

Since conflict is an inevitable part of life, and feelings will be injured from time to time, it's important to practice and model forgiveness as a tool for reconciliation. Asking for forgiveness and offering it to another is a powerful step toward healing. When we hold on to our bitterness and anger, we do not punish the one who has injured us, but continue to punish ourselves. Forgiveness does not have to mean forgetting what happened or condoning the actions of another person (particularly if the transgression was an egregious one). However, forgiveness can free us from continuing to be a prisoner to the pain that was caused.

Modeling forgiveness for our children may be challenging, particularly if this is not something that comes naturally to us. However, if we are able to confront our own resentments and let go of them, then we are able to show our children how to find forgiveness by example. When they see us let go of our grudges and forgive others, they are more able to learn to do this themselves.

Asking for forgiveness from our children when we make mistakes, verbally lash out at them, or engage in contradictory behavior is also a powerful tool for teaching children that we all do things we regret and that we can make amends. Being forgiven can also be freeing, particularly if we have been weighed down by guilt. Saying "I'm sorry" may sometimes be the hardest thing to do, but it can also be the greatest gift we can give to someone—or ourselves.

Teaching children about forgiveness also means allowing children to have the space and time to vent their feelings and express some of their hurt and anger. True forgiveness involves letting go, but this is a process and cannot be done effectively if children are taught to bury their feelings and just go on with their lives. Instead, we can help them to verbalize their feelings and find safe ways to vent their anger (such as punching a pillow).

While we can encourage our children to forgive, we cannot insist that they do so. When we tell them that they can choose to remain angry, we can also explain that holding on to this anger does not hurt the person who caused them harm, only themselves. Inviting them to confront the offender with non-judgmental words or asking their permission to pursue transgressions (such as bullying) with the offender's family or school can help them reach resolution and move toward forgiveness. Finally, expressing your thoughts about what causes people to do hurtful things may also help them to understand situations in which the offender herself was in pain and lashed out. Or, in the event that the hurtful action was not intended by the offender, you might say, "I'm not sure that Billy knew that was your favorite toy, and even if he did, it looked to me as if he didn't mean to break it, only that he wasn't sure how to use it properly. Perhaps if you told him how sad it makes you to see it broken, he may learn how hurt you are feeling and tell you that he is sorry."

Violence in Play and Entertainment

Another way to help your children learn about peacemaking is to consider the messages of peace or violence that come into your home through stories, movies, television programs, toys, video or computer games, and musical recordings. What should you do if these messages are contrary to what you would like your children to learn? Nancy Lee Cecil, in the book *Raising Peaceful Children in a Violent World*, suggests that you share the reasons why you feel the violent messages are inappropriate and ask your child or youth to think about how the situation being depicted could be altered for a more peaceful resolution. Sometimes using these situations as learning opportunities can be more beneficial than simply banning images of violence from the home.

As parents, we must often make unpopular decisions. Although we wish to treat our children with respect and affirm their positive natures, it is also up to us to set limits and create boundaries. If violent video games and toys are a line you just cannot cross, you need not feel bad for refusing to go there. By being consistent and setting limits, we teach children how to set limits for themselves. They may not appreciate our actions at the time we refuse to allow the toy or game, but someday they will look back and realize we had their best interests at heart.

Jen Pots describes the dilemma faced by many parents: "This area of play always causes me stress: Do I let him? Do I discourage? Do I educate? Do I leave it alone? Will I ever be okay with it? I've tried playing dinosaurs that love each other and to his credit, he appeased me as long as he could stand it, then he had one attack the other."

Mary Beth Schillinger, another Unitarian Universalist parent, has spent much time pondering the issue of toy weapons. "Prior to becoming a mother, I was active in a community effort against war toys. It seemed really obvious to me back then, black and white. . . . Now I'm much more confused. I see a lot of gray."

If you don't forbid aggressive or violent games and toys in your home, there is no need to believe you are raising the next generation of warmongers. A number of child development experts are coming to believe that some aggressive play is universal, particularly for some boys, and that it actually relieves stress. Aggressive play lets children grapple with issues of right and wrong, see good triumph over evil, and act out aggressive feelings in a safe way.

Penny Holland, a senior lecturer in early childhood studies at London Metropolitan University, has studied the behavior of boys in preschool settings. She determined that weapons and superhero play represent a developmental need for many of these children. If left to play on their own, the boys agreed on rules for the rough play. If boys for whom aggressive play meets an important need are repeatedly told that their play is inappropriate, they may internalize an impression of themselves as "bad" or "wicked." This may actually push them down the road toward later violent or aggressive behavior in non-play settings.

Similarly, some theorists suggest that violent television programs may have a positive purpose for some children. Such programs allow them to experience the human emotions that we are usually taught to deny: fear, greed, power hunger, and rage. Some children are drawn toward violent television programs and movies, just as some are drawn toward aggressive play or scary stories that may make an adult shudder.

Ultimately, parents have to go with their own instincts when determining whether violent toys, games, television shows, and music are acceptable. One key might be to look at not just the presence of violence, but how the situation is resolved. For instance, many people feel that the popular computer game *Grand Theft Auto* glorifies violence and sends the message that it is okay to abuse women and murder people. In contrast, the game *Resident Evil*, while also violent, promotes fighting off evil undead forces to save another human being from danger. Likewise, storybooks about pirates and soldiers don't have to be summarily discarded. Consider the messages that are communicated through the medium and how those messages fit with the values that you live every day and model for your children.

Violence in the Larger World

Although learning about being peaceful begins in the home, children quickly learn how little peace there is in the world outside their doors. For Unitarian Universalist children who are raised with peaceful aspirations, this can be especially disheartening.

It is not possible to shelter our children from the awful things that happen in the world and, in some cases, in our own neighborhoods, at least not completely. They are bound to come into frequent contact with disturbing news, given the current climate of instant global communication.

Children are incredibly resilient. Even youngsters who have grown up under some of the most terrible conditions, such as war, abject poverty, and violent crime—or have been subjected to horrific experiences of physical and sexual abuse—nonetheless can grow up to become healthy, loving adults. Those who have been most successful despite growing up amidst these kinds of conditions frequently credit their community of faith for helping them to believe in themselves and having at least one positive role model to encourage them.

Helping children understand violence and conflict not only prepares them should they ever be faced with such situations, but can also be instrumental in preventing future violence and conflict. Children have a pretty clear understanding of human nature—more than adults realize—and they have a tendency to see past the political polarization that so often muddles the peace process.

Children need to understand that with real-life violence, there is no "good guy" or "bad guy"—there is only conflict that has gotten out of hand. This may be hard for young children to grasp, since they are concrete thinkers whose idea of morality is that good behavior is rewarded and bad behavior is punished. Once children become "law and order" oriented in their morality, they want to categorize every conflict as a situation in which one group is breaking the rules and the other group is not. However, war and international conflict are rarely that simple. It may be helpful to remind children that everyone does good things and bad things, but killing or torturing people because of their race or religion is never right.

Talking about the inequality and injustice that often lead to conflict and war, including horrendous tragedies like genocide, can be daunting and should be determined by the child's age and maturity. Certainly teens should become aware not only of the atrocities that are being committed in the world, but also the social, economic, and political situations that led to these events. Parents can also help youth understand that conflicts occur in stages and that intervening at an early stage may prevent horrendous atrocities, if not halt the violence altogether.

Conflict usually starts with disagreements that can be recognized and accepted. In more advanced stages, people begin taking sides and become willing to associate only with those who think like they do. The people who are taking sides see the "other" group as the problem, believing that if the others would just see things their way, the conflict would be easily resolved. If the conflict continues to escalate, then each group begins to want to see the other group suffer, be ostracized, or even be eliminated. At this point the conflict has moved beyond the issue that caused the initial divide. It is now viewed as a moral issue, with each side thinking of the other as "evil." This is when the danger of genocide can occur. Only by remembering and learning from past atrocities, and by fighting denial and revisionism, are we able to work toward prevention and become a more just and humane society.

Humans have a natural tendency to react to horrific acts of violence with the desire to lash out and punish the perpetrators. People who are angry or frightened often feel that fighting back puts them in control of the situation or will somehow alleviate their pain and anger. While retribution may be a normal response, it exacerbates an already tragic situation. Children, in particular, may have difficulty channeling their anger and hurt feelings in appropriate ways and can easily pick up on adults' desire for revenge. We must help our children understand that violence and hate are never acceptable ways to express anger. It may help to remind them that justice and retribution are not the same: retribution breeds more violence, anger, and resentment, whereas justice halts the cycle of violence and brings the perpetrators to task for their actions.

We can communicate to our children that war and violence are choices, not the only solutions to conflict. Throughout history, people have found ways to live together in peace and harmony. Even nations that were once at war with one another have discovered ways to peacefully coexist.

We can also let our children know that we all need to be part of the solution—that peace really does begin with us. In the article, "Talking to Children About War," Naomi Drew suggests asking your children "what they think your family can do to create more peace personally and globally. If their ideas sound realistic, help them formulate a plan for social action; if not, talk them through to a reasonable and do-able project that they can get involved in."

To teach older children and youth about the complex issues involved in war and peace, invite them to go through a newspaper, cutting out headlines that suggest peace or violence. Then encourage them to "rewrite" the ones that suggest violence so that there is a peaceful resolution to the conflict.

Just as with teaching other values, the careful selection of stories, poems, songs, movies, and TV programs can communicate your ideas about a peaceful world. Presenting stories of how people (real or imagined) have actively worked for peace can plant seeds of possibility in the minds of children and youth. Pay close attention to the messages about peace and justice that are communicated through music, video games, and other media, and encourage children and youth to challenge instances where injustice and hatred prevail.

The Interdependent Web

Long before "going green" became fashionable and recycling commonplace, Unitarian Universalist families have been appreciating our connections to the environment and doing a variety of activities to make our world a better place. With our seventh Principle, "respect for the interdependent web of all existence," we spell out our duty to be caretakers of the earth, its living creatures, and all its resources. Whether we are gardening, recycling, composting, or clearing hiking trails of litter, many of us are actively caring for the earth. At the same time, we are teaching our children a genuine love of nature and helping them understand the spiritual gifts that nature gives us.

Hiking

Like many parents, Linda Lawrence of Illinois makes it a priority to walk in the woods with her children during different seasons of the year to call their attention to the cycles of nature. For many of us, hiking in a natural area can be a sacred experience. However, when children come along for the journey, we may need to adjust our expectations. Taking a silent five-mile hike through the woods can be a wonderfully meditative experience for an adult, but a nightmare for an eight-year-old. Even though the same child might run the same distance playing soccer or tag with friends, being forced to walk mile after mile with no end in sight can feel like a chore.

And then there are the issues of focus and attention span. For many young children, it is not the destination that is important, but the journey itself. If that is also your goal for the experience, there is less potential for conflict. However, if the plan is for your family to reach a wilderness campsite by a certain hour, frustration is bound to manifest itself every time a child stops to examine a spider web or a worm wriggling across the path. Allowing enough time to accommodate such pauses can help prevent irritation. So can changing your own perspective and taking a look at the world around you with the wonder of a child. Everything is so new and different for children that they can't help but be excited by the experiences that greet them. When we are intentional about sharing their wonder with them, we feel a new sense of joy about the natural world ourselves.

Since elementary-age children may have both a short attention span and a low boredom threshold, you may need to create diversions to avoid what Steven Boga, author of *Camping and Backpacking with Children*, calls "a veritable whinefest." Boga recommends tapping into the child's imagination with a treasure hunt. Children can be given a list of things to look for (a yellow leaf, a smooth rock, a feather) and either take pictures of them, sketch them in a notebook, or check them off the list as they are discovered. Playing games such as "I Spy" or "Twenty Questions" and singing trail songs such as "This Land Is Your Land" or "She'll Be Comin' Round the Mountain" can also encourage children with tired legs to keep moving. Frequent stops at points of interest and sharing thoughts about what is seen along the way can keep older children interested and create opportunities to absorb the many sights, sounds, and experiences of nature.

Giving older children their own pack to carry (with a minimal amount of items in proportion to their size) lets them feel they are contributing to the family venture. Pay attention to their energy level and attitude and avoid pushing them too far, too fast.

Hiking and backpacking trips are also an opportunity to teach children and youth about leaving as little mark on the natural world as possible. Having to carry out any trash you generate is a concrete reminder of how much we perpetually dispose of and encourages conservation. In many national parks and nature preserves, visitors are also requested to "take nothing but pictures." Children are natural collectors and will want to keep every pine cone, rock, and special twig they come across. Encourage them to appreciate everything they see, but leave it all where it is for others to enjoy. You might also invite them to think about what the forest would be like if everyone who came through it took some things with them.

Creative parents have used hiking experiences to share history with their children. You can inspire their imaginations by encouraging them to think about the Native Americans who may have once hunted in these woods, or the fur traders who forged trails to sell their wares, or the explorers who traveled this way for the very first time. Children can pretend they are explorers mapping out the terrain or hunters moving silently through the forest so as not to scare away the game.

If you don't know the history of the area, make up "pretend" stories and encourage your children to do the same. Little glens can become fairy havens, and an abandoned bonfire site might have been left behind by the lost tribe of the woods. Play games such as "I wonder . . ." in which you imagine what might have happened in this nature spot. Encouraging children to appreciate nature and develop their imaginations invites wonder and deepens their innate spirituality.

If you don't have time or opportunity to hike or backpack in the woods with your children, a simple walk in a nearby park or around the neighborhood can give you the chance to explore our world and take note of the changing seasons. Let young children pick dandelions and blow the seeds to the wind; show them how many different kinds of leaves there are; point out how the squirrel scampers up the tree and then jumps from limb to limb as if flying. Even short walks together as a family offer a gentle, relaxing time for sharing thoughts and listening to one another.

Camping

For families who want to take the experience of hiking one step further, the rewards of camping together can be immense. Many a reluctant parent has discovered just how well even young children take to camping and how our connections to nature are enhanced by leaving civilization behind for a time to sleep under the stars.

Most family camping trips intermix planned activities, such as hiking or fishing, with the many chores of camp life, such as preparing meals and washing dishes. But children should have plenty of opportunities to just "be" in nature as well. This may be a new experience for some children, whose schedules are often carefully choreographed with lots of enrichment activities. However, even children who are at first uncomfortable with unstructured time will eventually come to appreciate such moments as the best part of their camping experience.

Camping offers families the unique opportunity to go on night hikes. Introducing your children to the natural world after dark lets them become aware of all the nocturnal activity that goes on in the world and perhaps catch a glimpse of animals seldom seen during the day, such as owls and coyotes. In *Sharing Nature with Children*, Joseph Cornell suggests that you can increase your chances of spotting nocturnal animals by waving a flashlight across open clearings and looking for the shine of their eyes. If you want to see night animals without having them see you, put a red filter or a piece of red cellophane over your flashlight lens, since these animals aren't able to perceive red light.

There is no substitute for a campfire when it comes to roasting marshmallows and nighttime storytelling. Keeping stories lighthearted and humorous is a good alternative to scary tales that could induce nightmares or cause nervous campers to startle at every sound outside the tent. Stories can also be collaborative activities. Try encouraging each person to contribute a sentence to the tale, or offer a list of words that must be incorporated into a group story.

Nighttime at camp is also good for stargazing. On a clear night, more stars will be visible to the naked eye than is possible in more urban areas. Lying on their backs, children can find constellations or create their own. Myths and legends that grew out of these sky pictures can be shared or invented by creative minds.

Whether you're hiking, stargazing, or just sitting together around the campfire, nighttime nature experiences can provide an opportunity for self-reflection and bonding. Shrouded in darkness, family members may communicate on a deeper level than they do normally, sharing ideas and thoughts that might not be spoken otherwise. Camping may even help children overcome fears of the dark.

Kathleen Carpenter, a Unitarian Universalist parent from North Carolina, took her sons camping every summer. She and her family also regularly volunteered on trail service projects. Now her grown sons both have careers in which they appreciate nature—one runs a hiking and backpacking business, and the other works on environmental management projects.

Tracking and Still-Hunting

During the daytime hours, parents can engage their children in tracking animals in the wild. According to Steven Boga, more than any other skill, tracking animals will make children feel like wilderness experts. He says the study of animal tracks—besides being lots of fun for children—is great awareness training, since it "forces children to tune into their surroundings, to look critically at nature, and to play in the dirt."

Boga suggests giving children a "track pack" filled with items that can help them track animals around the campsite or on a wilderness trail. These track packs should contain a notebook and pencil, a tape measure or ruler, a magnifying glass, popsicle sticks for marking tracks to revisit later, and tweezers along with a few plastic sandwich bags for collecting evidence.

The best time to look for animal tracks is in the evening or early morning, when the sun is low on the horizon. When you find animal tracks, encourage your children to measure the length and width of each impression and the distance of the animal's stride. They can record the results in their notebooks along with a sketch of the tracks. Invite the children to guess what animal the tracks belong to. If you have a book of animal tracks available, they can compare the tracks to the pictures in the book.

Besides looking for prints, older elementary-age children can learn to discover other signs that reveal the presence of animals. These signs might include nests or burrows; trails or runs used to access water, food, and nesting sites; and the scratches that many animals leave behind when searching for food, climbing trees, or digging burrows. When animals pass under or beside an obstruction in their path, they may rub against it, leaving a telltale mark. Similarly, as animals move through plants and bushes, they may leave behind broken, torn, or trampled leaves or branches.

Joseph Cornell describes an activity known as still-hunting that was widely practiced by Native American youth. A young man would go to a place he knew well and felt attracted to, then sit down and let his mind settle into a still and watchful mood. If he had inadvertently caused a disturbance among the creatures around him, he would wait patiently until the area around him returned to its normal, harmonious routine. Then he would be completely still to observe and learn the movements of the animals in the forest.

Cornell suggests that when teaching children and youth still-hunting, we should encourage them to let their sitting place choose them, as the Native American boys did, with the understanding that one may be intuitively guided to a specific place in order to learn a certain lesson. The still-hunter must remain motionless, not even turning a head, so that the natural world goes on just as it does when no one is there. Cornell encourages still-hunters to feel that they are actually a part of the natural surroundings: "Mentally move with the shimmering leaves, or dance with the butterfly as it darts and dodges through the air. Because you are still, curious animals may come close for a look at you."

Gardening

Since most of the food that makes its way onto our dining tables comes in colorful packages produced in factories and purchased in grocery stores, it is not so easy for parents to illustrate the web of life. But having a garden in your backyard or a share in a community garden where your family grows tomatoes, green beans, and zucchini helps children understand that much of our food comes from nature. They can witness firsthand how the food that sustains us is grown in the rich soil of the earth, nurtured by the sun's rays, and drinks in water through thirsty roots. From a tiny seed, they can watch the miracle of life sprout and grow until it blossoms and brings forth fruit.

As anyone who truly loves gardening will tell you, gardening is more than physical exercise that gets you and your children out in the fresh air to tend plants. There is something richly spiritual about the entire process, from tending the soil to harvesting the vegetables or fruits that can then be enjoyed straight from the vine or prepared in the kitchen.

When we garden with our children, we also teach them to respect plants as living things and to recognize the many different varieties of plants that exist. They learn that plants have a purpose, and therefore understand that life itself is meaningful. This interaction with the natural world can help a child discover his own purpose. Just the idea of belonging to something larger than themselves can make children feel more valuable and nurture their spiritual lives.

You don't need a lot of land to share a love of gardening with your children. A few pots or planters can serve as container gardens, and herb garden kits can be grown on the kitchen windowsill. The growing popularity of community gardens allows people in even the most urban environments to grow fresh fruits and vegetables.

Most children have a natural affinity for digging in the dirt and love to water plants. They can also help with weeding, although young ones will need help distinguishing the weeds from the tender plants we are trying to grow. In fact, when gardening with preschoolers, you can consider yourself lucky if you end up with any bounty for your table. At this age, it is more about the process than the product. Young children may spend most of their time exploring the bugs that make their home in the dirt or watching worms wriggle their way through the soil. To encourage a love of gardening at this age, be flexible about what constitutes a garden. Instead of neat rows of tomatoes, it might feature a jagged and jumbled mix of lots of different plants. There should also be room for digging holes and discovering what happens when we move stones and sticks.

Elementary-age children can pick out seed packets, make signs for their seedlings, and tend their own gardens. They are mainly interested in the planting and harvesting parts of the gardening process, but should be encouraged to do some regular weeding, at least for a few minutes at a time. Even at this age, digging up bugs or making holes in the dirt and flooding them with water are immensely fascinating.

Salad greens such as endive, kale, spinach, lettuce, and chard require little effort to grow and can be planted and harvested in the spring. Radishes and strawberries also have a quick turnaround and produce early—a good choice for impatient youngsters looking for results. Among plants that last through the summer, most children prefer ones with huge blooms (like sunflowers) or tiny vegetables (like cherry tomatoes). Children also love plants with textured leaves, such as wooly lamb's ears and prickly coneflower, and vegetables with unusual colors, like speckled beans, yellow pear tomatoes, and red carrots. Scent also adds to the gardening experience. Plants such as lavender, rosemary, basil, and sage have powerful fragrances that can be enjoyed merely by walking though the garden.

There is also something special about attracting butterflies to your garden. The plants butterflies like best include monarda, milkweed, dill, parsley, and thistles. If you plant a butterfly garden, include some flat stones for the butterflies to rest on, intermixed with their favorite plants to take nectar from and lay their eggs on.

Attracting Birds and Other Wildlife

Many people place bird feeders in their backyards or on their windows or balconies. However, for those who want to do more to attract and care for birds, developing a bird sanctuary may be the key. As with gardening, you don't need a large plot of land to make a space inviting to birds. A few simple ingredients will create the necessary environment. A bird-friendly landscape provides the right habitat for nesting, eating, and engaging in social activities.

Trees provide a natural setting for nests and perching. To attract the greatest variety of birds, provide several types of deciduous and evergreen trees. Berry bushes and flowering plants allowed to grow wild are very appealing to birds and provide a food source.

Having some sort of birdbath is essential. Birds need water for drinking and bathing and prefer to nest and eat where there is a water source. This could be a traditional birdbath or a tiny pond made from a shallow plastic bowl snugly placed in a hole. Be sure to locate any ponds or bird baths away from trees, bushes, and areas accessible to cats. Placing a few bricks or large stones in any water source more than an inch and a half deep will provide a perch for tiny birds. Once your bath or pond is in place, fill it with fresh water each day.

Wild birds rely primarily on natural food sources, such as insects and seeds, but most will enjoy the convenience of a bird feeder. A feeder keeps the seeds dry during rainy days and won't let them blow away in the wind. Smaller feeders are easier for children to hang, but may be harder for them to fill without getting seeds all over the place. Children can easily refill a larger feeder if an adult takes it down and hangs it back up. Bird feeders should be placed in or near a natural shelter such as a tree or hedge, but out of the reach of squirrels, who will also want to enjoy the food source. For easy viewing, place the feeder near a porch or window.

Most birds will nest in trees or bushes, but some prefer a more secure, windproof site and will want a birdhouse available. Bird-houses should be installed away from natural predators and in an open space away from the house, trees, and large bushes. Some birds, such as purple martins, are highly social and like to build their nests close to other birds. Placing a martin house in your yard may be costly, but it will attract many martins, swallows, and swifts—all of whom eat hundreds of mosquitoes a day.

Appreciating Nature

In your own yard or a nearby park, there is a whole world of insects, birds, and small mammals to be discovered and observed. There is a whole lot of dirt that can be dug up to explore what the soil feels and looks like and what creatures live within it. There are trees that can be identified and named and observed throughout the seasons. Perhaps there are ducks at a nearby pond, swimming or nesting or searching for food.

When we share our own love of nature with children, they cannot help but join in our enthusiasm. Children are instinctively drawn to the wonders of nature, and when we encourage their observations and offer our own, we help them develop a lifelong love of the natural world.

Joseph Cornell tells us that every question, every comment, every joyful exclamation is an opportunity to communicate our own appreciation of nature to our children. When we encourage children's curiosity about the world, we inspire wonder and teach them about the amazing elements of life. Since there is life all around us, growing and blossoming and thriving, there is always more to see and explore. And since young children have a natural tendency to fully immerse themselves in whatever captures their attention, we can join them in watching even quite ordinary things with close observation. We can ask our own questions to spark their imagination and offer interesting facts to add to their sense of amazement. When we nurture our own curiosity and wonder about the world, we not only teach our children to love nature, but give them an opportunity to metaphorically touch the mystery of life itself.

Protecting the Environment

A love of nature easily translates into a desire to protect and care for the earth. This opens the door to family environmental projects. In many families, it is the children who have initiated energy-saving measures or recycling efforts in the home. In other families, parents may take the lead, but children are more than willing to contribute their part to sustain life on this planet.

For Liz Grimes and her family, taking care of the earth "is just part of our daily activities. We compost, we respect the cycle of nature, we try to protect the earth and learn about the life that we share with other creatures. We also talk at great length about major events in the world that impact our earth." For the Gressler family in Virginia, being "green" is a spiritual practice. Christine Gressler says, "Teaching our kids about caring for the earth is one of our greatest spiritual and ethical priorities."

Look for everyday opportunities to teach children how our actions affect the planet and all the living beings on it. Point out that when we generate trash, it has to go somewhere; it doesn't just disappear. Then see how much waste your family can eliminate by recycling, composting, and using fewer disposables. Talk about how chemicals affect the environment, then let your children help you make earth-friendly cleaning products from natural ingredients like vinegar, lemon juice, and baking soda.

You can also encourage your children to select an environmental cause that they wish to raise money for through special projects. According to Conservation International, donations from children in twenty-two countries helped establish the Children's Eternal Rainforest in Costa Rica, where more than forty thousand acres have been preserved since 1989.

Some families combine vacations with environmental volunteering. Conservation groups and other organizations always need helpers. One family spends vacation time searching for sea turtle tracks in order to mark nesting spots so that the endangered turtle's eggs can reach full maturity. Another family has taken time to scan the sky for hawks, eagles, and falcons during migration projects. Families can pick up trash on beaches as part of the Ocean Conservancy's annual International Coast Cleanup on the third Saturday of September. Through the Nature Conservancy, families can spend a working vacation clearing nonnative plants, planting indigenous ones, spreading mulch, and doing other tasks to improve natural areas. National parks need volunteers to plant or maintain gardens, clean up campsites, and return streams and trails to their natural state.

However, you don't have to leave your community to get involved in an environmental project. Many cities and towns organize volunteer projects to clean up rivers, tend community gardens, "adopt" roads, or clear brush for a newly created bike trail. Any time your family takes a walk or visits a nearby park, you can pick up trash to care for the environment right in your own neighborhood.

God and the Bible

Whether you are a theist, deist, pantheist, or atheist, you will inevitably face questions about God from your children. After all, God is mentioned in television programs and popular music, thanked by celebrities for their success, and worshiped by thousands of families every Sunday in churches all around the world. Unless children have absolutely no contact with the outside world, they will formulate ideas about the nature of the divine, whether or not you discuss God with them. The question then becomes: From whom do you want your children to learn about God, and what kind of God do you want them to learn about?

Images of God

In *Religious Literacy*, theologian Stephen Prothero reveals that nine out of ten adults in the United States believe in God. Although some of these people may not describe their God image in a traditional way, the vast majority do. According to Prothero, a full forty percent of Americans call themselves evangelical or "born-again" Christians.

In the major monotheistic religions of Judaism, Christianity, and Islam, God is viewed as a father figure—sometimes an angry, punishing father; sometimes a loving, forgiving father. But as Anne Carson points out in *Spiritual Parenting in a New Age*, with the huge number of children being raised in single-parent households, "a very large proportion of children literally have no concept what a loving father is, just as an only child can only wonder what it might be like to have brothers or sisters." However, since young children's notion of gender is still fluid, they can conceive of God as a loving parent without designating a particular gender. So although it may be hard for young children, with their concrete thinking, to understand God as a metaphor for love, peace, goodness, or the universe, they can understand a genderless being who loves them unconditionally. And perhaps when they are still young and in the early stages of faith development, this is the best that freethinking parents can hope for.

Many agnostic, atheist, or humanist parents are dismayed to hear their children profess belief in God, as if they have somehow failed in their attempts to teach independent thinking and skepticism. However, the reverse is true. When we teach Unitarian Universalist children to think, question, and observe, they cannot help but conclude that there must be an anthropomorphic deity. As with Santa Claus, the evidence seems overwhelming. Our children hear about God in the conversations of adults, in songs, in movies and television programs, and from their playmates.

Because children start out viewing their parents as all-powerful, it is not hard for them to make the leap toward understanding an all-powerful God as a parental figure. According to Rabbi Harold Kushner in *When Children Ask About God*, once children learn that their parents are in fact imperfect human beings, they eagerly fasten onto the idea of God as the superparent, capable of all things. This belief that God is in control of the universe, that things don't just happen randomly, helps children feel secure.

Unintended Messages

Intuition and perception also play primary roles in faith development for children of this age. Because of their egocentric thinking, young children will project their own meanings onto events without questioning whether or not those thoughts are accurate.

For example, a young child who overhears an adult refer to a tornado as "an act of God" may associate storms with the anger of a divine being. The next thunderstorm with high winds could be quite terrifying for him—especially if the child is feeling guilt over some wrongdoing. Suddenly this child's "irrational" fear of thunderstorms does not seem quite so irrational. In fact, Kushner says that even telling a child "God sees everything we do" can induce fear and guilt.

However, a child's belief in God can have positive effects as well. Marietta McCarty, author of *Little Big Minds*, points out that "most children are stimulated when learning expands to include the unknowable." When children realize it is possible to believe in things that cannot be proven, they can become enthralled with the concept of faith. Children are able to embrace the mystery surrounding the divine because they find the whole world mysterious. In fact, children have been disappointed, hurt, and confused when they are given the impression that any inquiries about God are unwelcome or forbidden.

Faith Development

As children grow older and move on to new stages of faith development, their ideas about the divine often change. Most children in liberal religious households will outgrow the conception of God as a father figure if encouraged to expand their thinking. During the elementary school years, when ideas of fairness and justice take center stage, children are likely to think of God as a judge who decides what is right and wrong.

Kushner says that around the age of ten, children will try to sort through everything they have heard about God. As they do, they begin to notice contradictions and impossibilities. At this point it becomes possible for them to recast their ideas about the divine into new terms that make better sense with their evolving understanding of the world. Parents can continue to encourage questions and offer their own views of the nature of the divine. Although children of this age still have trouble understanding abstractions, they are able to conceive of divine metaphors or to develop an idea of God as present in all living things or the entire universe.

This new way of thinking about the divine reorders a child's entire world. Kushner explains, "When the older child asks about God, I think he is really worried about whether the all-too-obvious loose threads of the world can be tucked into an orderly pattern." In contrast to younger children, who are mainly concerned about themselves, older children want assurance that the world treats everyone fairly in accordance with reliable standards of right and wrong.

The arrival of adolescence brings a move away from concrete thinking, opening up even more possibilities. Once abstract thinking develops, anthropomorphic images of God can be reexamined and new images created, even as youth begin to accept those mysterious depths of the universe that may be unknowable.

On the other hand, anthropomorphic images are still appealing to youth. James Fowler asserts in *Stages of Faith* that most, if not all, adolescent religious conversion involves recognizing the hunger youth have for a personal God—one who knows, accepts, and confirms their deeply held beliefs about themselves and affirms their emerging self-identity. This idea of God-as-Best-Friend is extremely appealing to youth, who struggle with forming an identity and finding their place in a group that accepts them for who they are. No wonder many evangelical Christian youth groups are so successful in recruiting teenagers when the message is "Jesus loves you, no matter who you are."

The Journey of Discovery

God has meant many different things to different cultures and people throughout history. Therefore, it makes sense for us to teach our children not only that the idea of God (or Goddess, Great Spirit, or a divine presence) is an individual, personal one, but that our personal notions of the divine may change over time as we grow and change ourselves.

Even if you have come to conclusions about God that are meaningful for yourself, you can teach your children that questions about the nature of the divine have not been answered to the satisfaction of a great many free thinkers. You can explain that most people's conception of the divine evolves as their faith development unfolds, and that there is much for us to discover as we grow and learn more about the world. You can suggest that our primary religious task is to wonder, to question, to explore new ideas, and to try to make sense of it all in a way that is relevant to us personally.

By exposing our children to many different ideas about God from various religious traditions, and by communicating our own views of God (both current and past), we can offer our children new possibilities that can help them grow spiritually. So perhaps the next time they are asked "Do you believe in God?" their answer will be "Which one?" or even "Yes," although their concept of God may be much different than the one their questioner had in mind. As Kushner says, "If we understand God to mean the Power that makes us feel in certain ways, the Spirit that causes us to know what Love and Hope and Compassion are like at all those moments when our spirits are in tune with the spirit of the universe, then we can believe that God is real—because we know that Love and Hope and Compassion are real."

Hell and Salvation

Sooner or later, every Unitarian Universalist parent faces the dreaded question "Are we going to hell?" or "Are we saved?" The question often comes after a child has been playing with or talking to another child who attends an evangelical Christian church, and the entire experience can be rather frightening. Since young children are such concrete thinkers with vivid imaginations, it is not difficult for them to conjure up the thought of a place of eternal torment full of fire and suffering.

As Unitarian Universalist parent Sharron Mendel Swain explains, "It starts when the church daycare that was the most economical option when the kids were little begins teaching about Jesus, God, sin, and salvation. For others, it starts when their kids hit first grade and a friend begins to share with 'our kids' that they are going to hell because they don't believe in Jesus, or don't believe in God, etc." For Sharron, who grew up Unitarian Universalist and is now raising her own children in the faith, this is a message she has heard repeatedly over her lifetime.

Another life-long Unitarian Universalist and retired minister of religious education, Ruth Gibson, remembers her mother saying, "Sometimes people use this Hell story because they think they have to frighten their children into being good. And if Julie's parents think she needs this story then we shouldn't take it away from her. But we don't need that story. In our family we are good because we love each other."

The bottom line is that our Universalist heritage speaks to us of a loving God who would not send people to such a horrible fate and our Unitarian heritage reminds us that people are basically good. Since these ideas are contrary to many of the teachings of evangelical or fundamentalist Christians—and taught to their children in Sunday school—we will need to be there for our children when they come to us for answers about Hell and if non-believers, or even those who don't attend the "right" church, will be sent there.

Religious Literacy

When asked, most of us agree that we would like our children to be familiar with the beliefs and practices of the many religions of the world. Yet we are not always comfortable teaching our children stories from the Bible. Perhaps it's because many of us rejected our childhood faith and don't want our children to go down the same path. We may worry that young children will take the stories literally and be frightened by some of them—Jonah being swallowed by a whale, God sending a flood to destroy the whole world. We may be concerned that our children will adopt beliefs that are contradictory to our own.

But if we neglect to teach our children Bible stories, we do them a great disservice. Unitarian Universalist children need to be familiar with the stories of the Jewish and Christian traditions so they can understand what so many of the people in the world take as a given. Stephen Prothero points out that "understanding Christianity and the Bible must remain the core task of religious literacy education, if only because Christian and biblical terms are most prevalent on our radios and televisions, and on the lips of our legislators, judges, and presidents." Not to understand these common reference points invites exclusion and possible ridicule.

More than one Unitarian Universalist child has been embarrassed to discover that everyone knows who Moses is but him. Annette Long explains her own confusion when her daughter Victoria asked her why there was "a man on a wooden T" while they were driving past a local Catholic church. "It took me a few moments to figure out what she was talking about, but I saw Jesus on the cross when I looked through my rear view mirror. That realization . . . made me cringe. I suddenly became aware of my failing in the religious/ spiritual training of my children. How could they, at age six, not yet know the story of Jesus and his death on the cross?"

Many of the people with whom your child will interact not only know Bible stories, but will assume that your child does too. One parent from California, who had wanted to shield her children from the violence in the Bible, was surprised when her oldest daughter was exposed to the story of Jesus' crucifixion at her supposedly secular preschool in conjunction with Good Friday. When the parent confronted the teacher about the nightmares her daughter had after hearing the story, the teacher was amazed. She had simply assumed that all children were familiar with the story of the crucifixion and resurrection. Clearly, if we do not teach our children stories from the Bible, then someone else will. By choosing to be the ones who share the information with them, we can make sure our children learn the stories in a loving, safe context and from a Unitarian Universalist perspective.

Furthermore, in a world where Christian fundamentalists cite the Bible as God's word and hold it up as sacred above all else, our children and youth need to be armed with the knowledge of exactly what these writings say. They need to understand the Bible so they can challenge the rigid interpretation of those who would use it as a basis for oppression.

Truth and Stories

If we look at the Bible through the lens of reason, we can easily show that it often contradicts itself or conflicts with our modern scientific understanding. But even if we do not believe that the events described in Bible stories actually happened, we can still find truth in them. Stories that are not literally true can reveal metaphorical truths about life. Jesus offered much of his advice and wisdom through parables because he understood the important role of storytelling in faith development. Other religious traditions also are ripe with wisdom tales—such as the Hindu creation story of the tortoise who had an elephant on his back to support the whole world—that explain the human condition or offer moral lessons, even though the events narrated seem literally impossible.

Therefore, we needn't dismiss Bible stories outright just because we don't think they really happened that way. Instead, Kushner suggests that we try to analyze them as we would a poem, by asking ourselves, "Is the point of this story true to life? Does it tell us something about the way the world really is?" The story of Cain and Abel thus becomes a parable of sibling rivalry and jealousy. The story of Jonah and the whale reveals the necessity of following one's calling despite misgivings. The nativity story can underscore the divinity in each child who is born. In this regard, we can think of the Jewish and Christian Bibles as containing stories not of literal events, but of inspired truths.

Human Flaws

Many parents are troubled by some of the immorality that appears to be condoned in the Bible. In a book that is so often touted as a guide to leading a good and moral life, we have to wonder about some of the actions of the people who are at the heart of its stories. At one point, Abraham denies that Sarah is his wife. Abraham is also willing to kill his son when commanded by God to do so. Jacob cheats his father and brother; Joseph tattles on his brothers, who get their revenge by selling him into slavery; and the great King David has a man killed because he desires the man's wife.

Kushner points out that by including such negative acts and immoral deeds, the Bible presents its leading characters as human beings, warts and all. This shows children that even great people have faults. "*You don't have to be perfect to be good*—that is one of the most important lessons the Bible has to teach a child—about himself, his parents and teachers, his friends," Kushner says. "A mistake, even a serious one, doesn't necessarily disqualify a person from the possibility of being a fine and decent human being."

The Interfaith Family

Fortunate is the family with two parental units who agree not only on matters of the heart, but also on matters of raising children spiritually. Fortunate also are the parents who are supported by extended family members who believe as they do, or at the very least accept their religious beliefs. But this is often not the case. Reconciling differing faiths is a daunting challenge that faces many Unitarian Universalist parents, for when loved ones disagree about matters of spirituality and theology, it can open up deep rifts and cause multiple conflicts.

Effects on Children

While it is possible to live in harmonious relationship with a person who does not share your theological and spiritual beliefs, it does present an additional parenting challenge. Since children are absorbent sponges taking in the attitudes, beliefs, and values of their parents, when parenting partners communicate contradictory messages, it can cause confusion.

All children need clarification of who they are. Religious practices—including the holidays that are celebrated and the rituals used to express beliefs—help form part of that identity. Children who are provided with a consistent, even if ever-evolving, faith tradition will develop a healthy relationship with religious ideas. When children are raised by parenting partners who have different theological beliefs, they are forced to incorporate two disparate and possibly conflicting religious identities.

Communicating our faith to our children usually involves more than just telling them what we believe. It also means sharing our intuitive responses to life and the practices we engage in, such as prayer, meditation, or other rituals. This combination of beliefs, feelings, and behaviors, according to faith development theorist James Fowler, is both consciously taught and indelibly imprinted by the patterns and expectations of our families and culture. The faith structure that emerges from the critical years of our childhood determines how we conceptualize and express what we find meaningful in life. In short, our faith development can underlie and permeate all future development—moral, psychological, and emotional—and as such is critical to who we are and what we will become.

While older children are generally able to handle the fact that two people can hold different and even opposing viewpoints, young children are less capable of understanding such discrepancies. And when theological and spiritual issues cause rifts between parents, children can conclude that the whole subject of religion is taboo.

Respect and Common Ground

As Anne Carson explains in *Spiritual Parenting for a New Age*, interfaith parents must respect one another's beliefs. "It is not merely confusing, but destructive to a child to see her parents sneering at one another's endeavors," Carson says. "It is the mixed signals, not the differences in belief, that damage the child's world view."

Focusing upon common ground and recognizing areas where you do agree with one another—such as your desire to raise healthy, happy children—can help parenting partners stay on track and not only keep their relationship solid but establish a framework for communicating with children about theological issues. It is also important for both partners to recognize that they do not have the ultimate truth. Although they can and should express their own beliefs, they must also leave room for the other parent's beliefs. Pete Wernick, in his essay "Parenting in a Secular/Religious Marriage," suggests that any comments about religion include the words "I believe or I don't believe." For instance, rather than stating "There is no God," a parent could say something like, "I don't believe there is a supreme being that dictates human affairs." Expressing beliefs in this way makes it easier to incorporate diverse theologies and spiritual expressions in the family.

For young children, who are literal thinkers, actual practices are easier to understand than intangible beliefs. In *Caretaking a New Soul*, Carson writes, "If the child wants to know, not unreasonably, why Daddy meditates and Mommy does not, or Mommy prays to Christ and Daddy does not, it can simply be explained that different people have different tastes, just as Mommy works in one occupation and Daddy another, and one parent takes tea with milk and sugar while the other doesn't."

At the same time, interfaith parenting partners should intentionally look beyond the outward signs of spiritual practices to the deeper meaning of their respective faiths. In doing so, they can often discover common values. Focusing on these areas of common belief can help them solidify their partnership and bridge their spiritual and theological differences.

Boundaries and Expectations

Establishing clear household behaviors and boundaries is a must for interfaith parents. If these expectations are set in advance, any conflict that arises is easier to manage because an agreement is already in place. Partners need only affirm or clarify their earlier agreement.

For example, Pete Wernick explains that he and his wife agreed not to display religious art, symbols, or statements in common areas of their home. Other agreements might set clear expectations for attendance at religious services or the celebration of religious holidays.

Some interfaith couples have developed and maintained a prenuptial pact on religious identity and communication issues. Others make such an agreement prior to the birth of a baby. But it is never too late to establish guidelines for how you will work in partnership with each other to raise your children in a multifaith home. Some of the issues that such an agreement might address are:

- Will the children attend religious services? Where? Who will accompany them? If one parent does not attend, what will be the explanation? If the children will attend religious services at two different institutions, how frequently will they attend each service?

- What religious holidays and holy days will be observed? How and where? Will there be any celebrations or rituals in the home related to the holiday? How will the nature and significance of the holiday or holy day be communicated?

- What rites of passages will be celebrated, and who will participate? Where will the rites take place? What rituals will be involved, and what is their significance? How will the meaning of the occasion be imparted?

- What portion of the family's financial resources will be contributed toward the support of religious organizations? Which religious organizations will be offered financial contributions? How much of your financial resources are you willing to commit to the expression of religious rituals, observances, and celebrations?

- What are each partner's priorities in terms of religious or spiritual expression? What, if anything, are you not willing to give up in the spirit of compromise? What do you feel you need to have in your life to express yourself spiritually?

Regardless of the content of your conversations and the result of your agreements, it is important to initiate communication on these issues and to keep talking about them. Susyn Reeve, an interfaith minister, suggests that parents approach these issues "as a way to deepen intimacy and create a deeper understanding of the place of religion and spirituality in your family."

Managing Conflict

In any committed relationship, the key to success is not the absence of conflict, but the ability of the partners to manage the conflicts that will inevitably arise. Parenting partners who have differing religious beliefs are likely to experience conflict, but that conflict does not have to damage the relationship or divide the family into warring camps.

In fact, couples who attempt to deny or downplay conflict tend to become emotionally distant, isolated, and secretly resentful, according to Paul Sanders and Susan Sances, clinical psychologists and interfaith parenting partners. They stress that persons who try to avoid conflict at all costs become vulnerable to unexpected outbursts or serious withdrawal. Conflict that goes unacknowledged can simmer and fester until it explodes in unhealthy and damaging ways.

This is especially true if one partner feels that his needs are continually unmet, or that her religious beliefs are viewed as less important than those of her partner. The agnostic parent may grumble, "Well, okay," when the pagan parent wants to hold a ritual for their daughter's coming of age, but secretly feel resentment that the daughter is being more heavily influenced by the practices of paganism. Likewise, the pagan parent who frequently forgoes special blessing rituals so as not to cause conflict with the agnostic partner is also in danger of feeling festering resentment.

Life transitions can cause the greatest conflict between interfaith parenting partners, even those who feel they have achieved a good balance of acceptance, respect, and communication. All rites of passage, from weddings to child dedications to memorial services, carry religious overtones that may make it necessary to reexamine previous agreements. This can be a good time to turn to others for help. If both partners attend a Unitarian Universalist congregation, the minister may be able to provide pastoral counseling and guidance for the family. Otherwise, it may be necessary to seek guidance from a psychologist or counselor who has experience working with interfaith couples.

The lessons about conflict we learn as children follow us into our adult lives and into our committed relationships. As Rev. Colleen McDonald explains, "We may subconsciously repeat the patterns and strategies we learned in our families of origin, or we may consciously make an effort to improve on the examples we were given. Either way, it is not unusual for a couple to discover they have different feelings about conflict and different ways of handling it." Since any conflict that touches on one's deepest values, beliefs, and aspirations can cause significant stress in a marriage, interfaith couples are particularly at risk. While couples may become more skilled at managing conflict over time, some find that they are just unable to work it out, and the stress that the conflict places on the relationship leads to irreconcilable differences.

After Divorce or Separation

The complications of raising children with a parenting partner who believes differently than you do is only compounded after a divorce or permanent separation. However, even parents who were unable to continue in intimate relationship with one another can come to agreements with one another and show respect for differing points of view.

If religious issues were not a major contention during the partnership before its dissolution, then it may be easier for a couple to communicate about how they will continue to raise their children religiously. During the discussions of property division, custody, and visitation, it may be necessary to make a point of expressing intentions and expectations around religious and spiritual issues. Otherwise, partners may be setting up themselves and their children for a lifetime of struggle, disappointment, and resentment.

In the book *Integrity*, Stephen Carter outlines three steps that are helpful to all divorcing parents, but especially those who will continue to raise their children in two separate faiths. The first step is discerning the right thing to do. For example, this may mean working with the other parent on a plan for raising the children actively in your two faith traditions. The second step is acting on what you have discerned, even at personal cost. This might mean respecting the other parent's religious beliefs, even when your son arrives in your atheistic home singing "Jesus loves me, this I know." The third step is saying openly that you are acting on your understanding of right and wrong. This helps to clarify your behavior. For example, if you feel that your former partner is undermining your attempts to raise your children with a sense of Unitarian Universalist identity, you can offer clear reasons for your objections.

Not every divorcing couple has the respect and ability to communicate effectively in order to make a co-parenting arrangement work. But when it comes to raising children spiritually, the only alternative is one parent dominating the theological education of the children while the other parent's faith takes a back seat. Despite their best efforts, some couples are simply unable to come up with an acceptable agreement that honors both sets of beliefs. In these cases, it may be necessary to consult with a professional mediator or psychologist, who can help draw up a plan for parenting in partnership.

Death and Grief

Even if a child does not experience the death of someone close to him, he will inevitably have questions about what happens after a person dies. Except for sex, there is possibly no other subject that our children are more frequently exposed to through popular culture and the media. But unlike in generations past, when experiencing death was a natural part of life, our children often have little or no direct experience of death until it strikes painfully close to home. And the images of death they are bombarded with through popular culture are often frightening, misleading, and unhealthy.

What we tell our children about death will depend mostly on their age and life experiences. Our own experiences, beliefs, feelings, and understanding of the meaning of life and death will also make a difference in what we say. Finally, since each situation we face is somewhat different, we may bring up different aspects of what happens after a person dies at different times. For instance, a discussion about death that is motivated by a news report or a television program doesn't carry the same emotional charge as explaining the death of a loved one or pet.

The Great Mystery

In talking to our children about death, the particular challenge for many Unitarian Universalist families is the absence of comforting answers. Because most of us aren't sure what happens after a person dies, we have a tendency to waffle when answering questions or attempting to explain our beliefs about death. Our children, however, are hoping we can offer them reassurance and wisdom, and can be quite confused when we have little to give them. By being truthful with them, providing emotional comfort, and validating their experiences, we can help our children understand and accept death as a natural part of life, and even find some meaning in their grief.

As Sophia Lyon Fahs and Elizabeth Manwell explain in *Consider the Children,* "Death confronts us starkly with the Great Mystery that enfolds all mysteries, the relationship between flesh and spirit, body and mind, the material and the immaterial." In witnessing the lifeless body, it becomes clear that without the "spirit" or essence of what this person was, the body appears to be merely a shell. The real question is whether the spirit can live on after the death of the body. Since this question cannot yet be answered on the basis of scientifically observed facts, it is an issue of faith. The job of sharing these issues of faith with children falls to parents, at a time when they may be longing for reassurance themselves.

When someone close to the child dies, the emotional distress is likely to make any thoughtful searching into the Great Mystery very difficult. Children rarely grieve in isolation; it is highly likely that others in close relationship to the child are also feeling the pain of loss. Shared loss affects each individual differently. Some people may be overwhelmed with feelings of guilt, loneliness, resentment, or even anger. Others may wallow in depression. Still others may not seem to grieve at all as they dive into work or tackle projects in the hope of avoiding their feelings of pain and sorrow.

But the reality is that nothing will cause us to question our faith like experiencing the death of a loved one. This is true for adults as well as children. Some theist parents have been disheartened to hear their children announce, "There can't be a God, because it makes no sense for God to let her die." Atheist or agnostic parents may be equally dismayed when they hear their child or youth express a new heartfelt belief in life after death or reincarnation as a result of having experienced a loss. Because it is the Great Mystery for which we have no answers, death has the power to challenge our thinking and compel us to examine the core of our beliefs. For parents experiencing grief, this process is multiplied tenfold, because we must also address the questions of our children and youth.

Young Children

To many adults, it may seem as if children under the age of five have a rather casual attitude about death. Since death appears so much like sleep, preschoolers cannot fully comprehend that it is irreversible and their loved ones will not return. And because they are such concrete thinkers, children will assume that any discussions about life after death mean that the physical body will come back to life.

In *Explaining Death to Children*, Earl A. Grollman suggests that children can comprehend death more easily if it is explained in terms of familiar life functions. For example, you could say that when people die, they do not breathe anymore, their heart stops beating, and they no longer eat, talk, think, or feel anything. In the case of pets, you might explain that "when dogs die, they do not bark or run anymore."

Since there is no right way to grieve, children, like adults, must find their own way through the process. You can be supportive by encouraging children to ask questions, listening as they sort out their feelings, and allowing them to be alone when needed. Sharing your personal feelings, without overburdening the child with your own grief, can help validate the child's experience. "I miss Grandma very much too," you might say. "We had fun when she came over for dinner on Sundays, and now we won't be able to do that anymore."

Telling children what has happened in a matter-of-fact way, without euphemisms or platitudes, may seem harsh, but it is necessary to avoid any confusion. Because young children are very literal, they are likely to misunderstand euphemisms about death. Any comparisons to sleeping should be avoided, or you may discover your child developing a terrible fear of going to bed at night or taking a nap.

Likewise, being told that a beloved grandparent has "gone away" may cause great anxiety the next time a parent goes on a business trip. Even comments about "being with God" can cause resentment and anger in the minds of young children, who may see God as selfish for having taken away their loved one. Because they do not yet fully understand cause and effect, young children may also make connections where none exists: "Grandpa was coughing before he died, and now Mommy is coughing, so maybe she will die, too."

Since their minds still struggle with reality and fantasy, lack a clear sense of cause and effect, and have an egocentric view of the world, it makes perfect sense to children that their personal thoughts or actions were the direct cause of their loved one's death. A child may feel a tremendous amount of guilt for having said or thought something mean, or imagine that if she had been a better person, her loved one might still be alive. The fact that the dead are often idealized and spoken of with great praise makes the guilt worse. As Fahs and Manwell point out, "A child afraid to tell his feelings hides them in the darkness of his own loneliness, where they may spread until they poison the inner life." This is particularly true when a sibling has died—the surviving child may develop a complex, persistent belief that had it been she who died, her parents might be less sad.

It is important to directly address a child's feelings of guilt, whether or not they are expressed verbally. Assure the child that he is not responsible for the death of the person or pet in any way. Stress the circumstances that led to the death, and reinforce how the child had no control over what happened—despite what he may have thought or even wished for.

Young children also struggle with understanding the permanence of death. Even though it may be difficult for the grieving parent, children may need to be given repeated explanations of the facts surrounding the death of a loved one, along with reminders that death is permanent. The reality of the death should be repeated calmly and matter-of-factly: "No, Lucy won't be coming to your birthday party because she died. Dying is forever."

Young children have difficulty naming their feelings and addressing them in productive ways. Behavior such as bedwetting, tantrums, or unusual moodiness often results from unaddressed feelings of guilt and anger. According to Mimi Doe in *10 Principles for Spiritual Parenting*, "Young ones do not have the articulateness or awareness to verbalize what's troubling them. Thus, many of their most heartfelt attempts at communication are expressed in a kind of code, in jokes or asides, in complaints or non sequiturs." It is often up to the parent to decode a child's questions, odd-sounding statements, inappropriate behavior, and aggressive acting out as a call for help. Often some form of creative outlet, such as music, pretend play, mask making, sculpting, or painting, can help children express their deep feelings. Physical release through sports, active play, or dancing can also serve to channel pent-up feelings in positive ways.

Some young children may show little immediate grief, appearing as if they are unaffected by the loss. However, it may be that they are not yet mature enough to work through a deeply felt loss. Children may express their grief in stages; as they move on to a new developmental stage, they will grieve as that stage allows them to. This prolonged grief process is a protective mechanism that allows children to work through their grief in more manageable ways. However, for parents who are grieving as well, it can be difficult to deal with a child's extended grief that seems to turn on and off at unexpected moments. While they may find it painful to have old wounds probed again and again, parents should realize that children need lots of patience, understanding, and support to complete their journey through this unfolding grief process.

Elementary-Age Children

During the elementary school years, children come to recognize death as a permanent condition. They often personify death, thinking of it as an almost malevolent presence. With their newfound understanding of cause and effect and their "law and order" moral sense, they see death as the great punisher of wrongdoing. Feeding this fear, even unintentionally, can create deep anxiety or depression in a child. Therefore adults should avoid moralizing about deaths that might have been prevented ("he should have known better than to swim out so deep").

Elementary-age children may develop a paralyzing fear of what will happen to them during and after death. They may imagine that they will experience a painful death or go to a frightening afterlife. They may fear being trapped in their dead body as it is buried in a coffin, or feeling the pain of being burned during cremation.

Guilt is a strong factor in the grief process of an elementary-age child. While he may no longer believe that his thoughts or actions directly caused a loved one's death, he may instead dwell on "ifs": "If only I had been holding Grandpa's hand, maybe he wouldn't have fallen down" or "If only I had gone over to Grandma's house like she asked, I would have been there when she had the stroke and could have done something to help her." As with younger children, you may need to be direct in communicating that your child is not at fault for the person's death. Stress that even if she had been present, there are some things we just don't have control over.

According to Barbara Coloroso in *Parenting Through Crisis*, children of this age may be obsessed with knowing the facts surrounding a death. If it was an accident, they might want to hear all the details: what direction the car was coming from, whether it was possible to see the truck before it hit. They may also ask questions about the decomposition of the body or how it is prepared for burial. Although you may find such details morbid or painful, they help children process what happened and understand the meaning of death. By accepting their natural curiosity and patiently answering their questions, you can help children with their grieving process.

The death of a sibling or a friend near the child's age brings home a sense of personal mortality that the death of a grandparent or pet does not. Children in this situation must struggle not only with their grief, but with the idea that they too might die at any time. This double blow can be devastating to a child, but the effect can be diffused somewhat by addressing the issue directly. If the death was due to an accident, emphasize that while accidents sometimes happen, we do all we can to keep each other safe. If the child died of an illness or other medical condition, reassure your child that he does not have this problem himself and will probably live a very long time. Adding that most of the time when something goes wrong with our bodies it can be fixed, but sometimes it can't, can help the child come to grips with what happened. Similarly, if the death was a result of violence, help the child understand that she is safe and that the likelihood of this happening to her is very small.

In the case of a violent death, it is natural for children to be angry at whoever was responsible. Emphasize that the authorities are doing everything they can to find and punish the perpetrator. Because focusing on their anger will only impede the healing process, children may need help coming to acceptance and perhaps eventually offering forgiveness.

Young Adolescents

With the arrival of early adolescence, death is finally perceived as universal, irreversible, and eternal. Rather than something imposed by an outside force, death is understood as a biological process.

While young adolescents have a greater understanding of the permanence of death, some of them may seem unaffected by it on the surface. Inside, however, they may be roiling with unexpressed emotions. Depending on their age, their relationship to the person who died, and the circumstances surrounding the death, they are likely to feel a mixture of emotions that could include anger, resentment, guilt, sorrow, and perhaps shame. Anger toward the deceased person may be repressed, compounding the feelings of guilt. Anger toward parents, siblings, or other friends for not being able to prevent the death may either be repressed or overtly expressed through impulsive, even violent, behavior.

It is also common for a young adolescent to experience a delay in the onset of her feelings. On hearing the news, the youth may not have an immediate emotional reaction. She may feel numb through the funeral or memorial service, and experience guilt for not feeling what she thinks she should be feeling. This delay is a normal way of protecting the self from the full onslaught of immediate grief. Eventually the force of grief will be felt—whether it is days or even weeks or months later. In the meantime, reassure the youth that we all grieve in our own way and in our own time, and that you will support her when she is ready to talk or has questions.

Because adolescents are likely to be moving into a new stage of faith development, the death of someone important to them will have a big impact on their evolving sense of self and their beliefs about the meaning of life. Like many adults, young adolescents wrestle with the deep "why" questions ("Why her? Why now? Why that way?"). Having opportunities to pose these questions and reflect on them with a trusted adult—a mentor, counselor, or good friend— may facilitate this process, especially when parents are themselves deeply affected by grief and unable to adequately be present to the young adolescent's needs.

Older Adolescents

Older youth will likely have an adult understanding of the finality of death and the fact that everyone will die, including themselves. However, they do not yet possess the coping mechanisms and big-picture thinking that maturity and experience provide.

Teens can react to death in a variety of ways. Some act out in anger; others deny their feelings. Adolescents tend to look toward their family for cues on how to cope. If they see you presenting a brave front, they may think they need to bury their emotions as well. Trying to do so can leave them feeling misunderstood, alien-ated, and even more angry. Teens also tend to seek out their peers for support and consolation. In general, adolescents who have a healthy and mature network of friends generally deal with loss in a healthier way.

As a parent who is also dealing with loss, you must strike a balance between meeting your own needs and those of your adolescent. Expressing your feelings related to the death can encourage your teen to open up about her own complicated thoughts and feelings. However, be careful not to overburden her with responsibility for your emotional well-being.

Even if your teen seems to be handling things just fine on the outside, offer your support and encouragement. If he doesn't want to talk about the loss, it doesn't mean that you're not needed. Sometimes the best thing you can do is just be present. Give your teen the opportunity to reflect on his own timetable. When he is ready to talk, simply listen and reflect back some of the things you are hearing, without offering advice or communicating how a person should or shouldn't feel.

After the death of a family member, some teens inappropriately try to assume adult responsibilities, such as shouldering financial obligations or "parenting" other members of the family. To safeguard against this, reassure teens that they are not responsible for adult concerns and need not try to fill the role of the deceased family member. Help them work through any feelings of guilt that may be kicking around in their brains.

Some youth will seek to embrace their angst, allowing the experience of death and grief to define their developing identities. According to Rev. Kendyl Gibbons, "There is a certain existential heroism and tragedy about living in the shadow of mortality, which teens in particular find quite romantic." They will eventually pass through the most dramatic form of this phase of their philosophical and spiritual development. But in the meantime, their romantic notions of mortality may be quite sincere and deeply felt. Embracing the inevitability of death may seem morbid, but teens are just attempting to accept their new understanding of mortality.

Some adolescents seek control over their mortality by taking unnecessary chances with their lives. Driving recklessly, jumping from high places, or playing "chicken" with a speeding train—and surviving the experience—give the illusion of control and help lessen fears about dying. However, teens who engage in physical risk-taking really do take their lives into their own hands. Alternatives like bungee jumping, skydiving, and roller coaster rides can provide the thrills of physical danger with far less actual risk.

Suicide

Since suicide is the third leading cause of death among people age fourteen to thirty-five, it is not unlikely for teens to experience the unique pain of surviving the suicide of someone they know. Suicide is not only sudden but disorienting. It leaves mourners feeling inadequate and betrayed. In the midst of their grief, they cannot escape the circumstances of the death. They feel shame at the stigma of suicide, guilt that they could not prevent it, and rage for being abandoned. In addition to the usual "whys" and "what ifs," they ask questions like "How could he do this to us?" and "Why couldn't she just talk to me?"

In this situation, as when coping with any death, parents must keep the lines of communication open. Listen to your teen without criticizing or judging. Responding with "You don't mean that!" when your teen expresses anger toward the person who died will only increase her guilt and shut down any further communication.

Sometimes grieving youth, driven by the deep emptiness they feel, express thoughts about not wanting to go on living. Even these statements require a nonjudgmental response. Acknowledge the feelings expressed behind the words: "Death is hard for us to deal with; it can make us feel so overwhelmed that we just don't know how we can bear it any longer."

Expressing such sorrowful thoughts is different from actually considering suicide. Signs that someone may be thinking of suicide include sustained lack of interest in favorite activities, behavior problems that show no signs of being resolved, withdrawal from family and friends, changes in sleeping or eating habits, neglecting personal hygiene, discarding or giving away treasured possessions, and engaging in risky behaviors or substance abuse. If you notice any of these signs, seek assistance from your minister and a qualified mental health professional who works with teenagers and grief issues.

Conflicting Beliefs

Inevitably, your child or youth will at some point encounter ideas about death that differ from your family's beliefs. Ideas about heaven, hell, ghosts, communicating with the dead, and reincarnation can hold a great deal of attraction, since they offer reassurance of continued survival after death and possible reunions with loved ones who have died. If such concepts are not part of your personal beliefs, how should you react when your child or youth brings them up? A good way to start is by reiterating your own beliefs about death and the possibility of an afterlife. You might also ask why your child finds these alternative ideas attractive. Were they stated by an important authority figure, such as a favorite teacher or a friend's parent? Instead of challenging or contradicting that person, you might explain again that although people have come up with many possible answers, no one really knows for certain what happens after a person dies.

In the case of youth, it may be particularly important to explore why certain ideas about death are so appealing. Do they merely provide a sense of comfort, or are they consistent with an evolving sense of faith development? If you casually dismiss these beliefs as unrealistic, you could unintentionally disrupt the process of belief formation. However, it is still possible to express your own beliefs while validating your youth's process of exploring options and looking at possibilities.

Some religious philosophies emphasize not the reward of an afterlife, but the importance of living this life to the fullest. Talking with children and youth about this idea, says Marietta McCarty in *Little Big Minds*, brings a spirit of peace that "comes with a realization that they can better deal with death by taking charge of life." While such an outlook does not erase the pain that accompanies any loss, it helps restore some sense of control. Although we usually cannot control death, we can exercise power over our lives and make them meaningful through the way we choose to live and the people whose lives we touch with our love.

Rituals of Closure

Because of their natural creativity and openness to expression, children can gain even more comfort and closure from rituals than adults do. Including our children in the planning of end-of-life ceremonies gives them the opportunity to do something concrete for the departed loved one and for themselves.

Whether or not they help with the planning, if children will be present for the funeral or memorial service, they should be prepared in advance for what they will likely experience. In particular, if there will be an open casket, explain not only that it will be possible to see the deceased person's body but what it might look like. Also describe how and when the casket will be closed, lowered into the ground, and covered up with dirt. With young children, it might be necessary to reflect again on what it means to be dead. Emphasize that the person will not wake up and can no longer think or feel. If children do not understand this, they may fear the person is being buried alive and will feel trapped or unable to breathe.

If there is to be a religious service, describe what will take place, particularly if children are not familiar with the rituals of the religious tradition. Provide details for any other routines that will be followed (we will light candles, people will tell stories about Grandma). Make a point of informing children that they may see people cry, and that this is okay; crying is one way that people can express their grief over the person's death. Also let them know that they will see other people who are not crying and that this, too, is normal. Hearing these expectations gives children permission to express their own emotions in whatever way feels natural.

Children sometimes have a hard time understanding what appears to be a party following the service. You can explain ahead of time that although we are sad when someone dies, we can't be sad all the time. We also need to be joyful as we remember the good times we shared with the person who has died. Knowing this also helps children realize that as life begins to return to normal, it's okay for them to be happy and enjoy themselves.

It's natural to think of a departed loved one on special days each year, such as the person's birthday or the anniversary of his or her death. Openly acknowledging, and even embracing, these special days serves to affirm the continuing process of grief and acknowledge the importance of the person in the lives of the living. A family might mark the occasion by sharing stories about their loved one, eating a favorite meal, or taking part in an activity that the person loved.

Lighting a candle to remember a loved one who has died can be a comforting ritual. In a Jewish tradition, families light a special candle, a *Yahrzeit* (or memorial candle), which burns throughout the twenty-four-hour day on the anniversary of a loved one's death. This ritual serves to recognize the importance of the date, acknowledges the feelings of loss that linger throughout a lifetime, and symbolizes the flame of life that once burned brightly and illuminated the lives of the loved ones who now mourn their loss. During rites of passage such as a wedding, coming of age ceremony, or child dedication, a candle can also be lit to acknowledge the special person who cannot be present physically, but is with the family in spirit.

The Cycle of Life

It is much easier to talk about death when we are not mired in grief over a loss. Exploring the natural world with our children offers opportunities to talk about life and death and the cycle that is experienced by all living things.

Some young children show intense curiosity about dead insects, birds, and animals. They may want to examine them closely or ask detailed questions about what happens to dead things. Children should never be made to feel guilty or embarrassed about their curiosity. If you communicate (intentionally or unintentionally) that talking about death is off limits, children will come to understand that death is something so horrible even parents can't talk about it.

Instead, use such teachable moments to help children reflect on how all life is part of a cycle. At the very beginning comes birth, followed by growing up, growing old, and finally death. Explain that all living things die, and when they do, they make room for new living things to take their place. Talk about how a fallen tree decomposes and becomes a source of new life even in death, or how dead birds and squirrels serve as food for scavengers. In this way you can offer your children the idea that life and death complement one another and are part of the natural order of things.

Sexuality and Love

Sexuality can be considered a basic part of our physical, emotional, intellectual, and spiritual lives. It is not just sex, but the roles, behaviors, and values that people associate with being male or female. It is evident in the clothes we choose to wear, the activities we choose to engage in, the ways we show affection to others, and the persons we are attracted to. It is the identity we internalize and the image we project to the world.

Children have different concerns and questions about sexuality at different ages. Young children are curious about words they don't understand and wonder about the miracle that brings new people into the world. Preteens and older youth spend a lot of time worrying about whether they are "normal." One of the most important messages we can give our teens is that it is normal to be different.

In *From Diapers to Dating*, Debra Haffner explains that there is a distinct difference between child sexuality and adult sexuality. Unlike the behavior of sexually consenting adults, which is directed toward orgasm or erotic feelings, most childhood sexual behavior is naïve and curious.

Biological Changes

Understanding the changes that puberty brings can increase children's comfort level. Knowing that these changes happen on an individual timetable of development can help ease any fears of being vastly different from other children.

Without placing an undue emphasis on physical attractiveness, parents can encourage their preteens to bathe more frequently and show them simple hygiene techniques. Girls in particular may be swayed by the images of women they see in magazines and music videos. Parents may need to encourage their daughters to select clothing that flatters their particular shape and size. Girls who are drawn to overtly sexual or revealing clothing should be encouraged to consider what image they wish to present to the world and how our clothing choices reveal messages about ourselves. Because she is choosing these clothes in part because of her belief that these images are what make females physically attractive, it may also be important to expose her to other images of beauty which do not involve overtly sexual or revealing clothing.

Adolescent girls and boys are curious about the opposite sex and sexual activity. While boys have long discovered their parents' or relatives' secretly stashed copies of *Playboy* and *Hustler*, these days many teens and preteens are turning to the Internet for sexual imagery. But images of sexuality on the Internet can be unhealthy and even damaging. To head off this behavior, actively communicate your desire that your youth not access online pornography or questionable websites, and offer other sources with more accurate information and positive messages about sexuality. One option is to enroll your youth in the comprehensive sexuality program for junior high youth, *Our Whole Lives* (OWL), developed by the Unitarian Universalist Association in conjunction with the United Church of Christ. The OWL program for grades 7–9 offers age-appropriate information on sexuality, including topics such as gender issues, sexual orientation, sexually transmitted diseases, and relationships, presented by trained facilitators in a safe context.

When your children reach puberty, you may find yourself shying away from showing them physical affection. When they were younger, it was easy for them to curl up on your lap for a quick cuddle; now the two of you seem to end up in an uncomfortable tangle of limbs. But if you suddenly give up all physical contact with your children, they will get the message that you no longer feel affectionate toward them, whether they consciously recognize it or not. On the other hand, your adolescents may attempt to assert their independence by refusing to be hugged, causing you to feel rejected. However, many of the same youth who shy away from hugs and kisses will appreciate a simple shoulder squeeze or hand rub.

Affectional Orientation

The experience of growing up bisexual, gay, lesbian, transgender, or questioning is unlike the experience of any other minority in the United States. (It has become increasingly common to refer to this broad category of orientations and identities with the acronym BGLTQ.) Compared to children of color, for example, BGLTQ adolescents are less likely to grow up with parents who are also members of their marginalized group. Straight parents who are raising a gay son cannot offer guidance based on their own experience of growing up gay. Instead, they may need to acquire a new mind-set as they learn how to be supportive and encouraging to their BGLTQ youth.

Parental support is essential if BGLTQ youth are to develop a positive sense of self. Since sexuality is interwoven with behavior, values, and beliefs, it is not possible to extricate sexuality from one's identity as a person of worth. BGLTQ youth must learn to accept the truth about themselves and, with the help of their parents, come to love themselves for who they are.

This is especially true for youth who are transgender. Even parents who accept their teenager's transgender identity may harbor a secret wish that their child could just fit in, since it would make life so much easier. Like all caring parents, they hate to see their child as the target of harassment and teasing and would prefer their youth not have additional burdens to carry. However, while the desire to protect children from the hardships of life is admirable, we cannot shield them from their own learning experiences. Besides, a parent's negative perceptions of the difficulty of living a transgender life may make adjustment and acceptance even more difficult for the child.

Research shows that BGLTQ youth who are forced to hide their true selves from the world are much more likely to engage in risky behaviors such as unprotected sexual activity, drug use, and alcoholism. Furthermore, although it may seem ironic, BGLTQ adolescents have twice the risk of unwanted pregnancy as straight teens. Some gay, lesbian, transgender, or questioning youth have heterosexual sex out of a desire to "cure" themselves, because they are not yet able to accept their true sexual orientation. Others may see developing a reputation for promiscuous heterosexual activity as an effective way of getting harassers off their trail. Some young women who identify as lesbian or transgender are raped, a violent and misguided act intended to teach them that they should be interested in boys. All this sexual activity creates a high risk of sexually transmitted diseases, in part because youth who don't feel good about themselves are less likely to protect themselves during the promiscuous behavior.

The need for parents to support their BGLTQ youth is clear, but it is not necessarily easy for them. While many straight people have trouble acknowledging it, deep within their subconscious they may have lingering beliefs and fears about sexuality. Some parents may feel it is perfectly fine for others to be BGLTQ, and may even have gay, lesbian, or bisexual friends, yet feel a deep sense of ambivalence or even discomfort when their own child announces that he is gay. Part of that discomfort is due to the way our society views sexuality when defining a person's identity. If you are attracted to the opposite sex, your sexual behavior is probably not viewed by others as a defining characteristic of who you are. But society tends to define the identity of BGLTQ individuals by their sexuality above all else. Because of that societal double standard, as well as unresolved issues and misunderstandings, even well-meaning and progressive-minded people may have uncomfortable feelings about BGLTQ sexuality. This is also why the term *affectional orientation* is sometimes preferable to *sexual orientation*—it places the emphasis upon love and affection and off of sexual expression.

Facts and information can help alleviate any ambivalence or discomfort parents may feel, as well as prepare them for educating other family members and friends about their child's sexuality and affectional orientation. They can also focus on keeping the lines of communication open and creating an atmosphere of acceptance for all kinds of diversity, including sexual identity.

Some straight parents, although supportive of their BGLTQ youth, feel sad because they fear there will be no grandchildren in their future. However, homosexuality does not preclude the possibility of having children any more than heterosexuality guarantees it. Affectional orientation does not prevent people from adopting a child if they choose to do so, and options such as in vitro fertilization, surrogate motherhood, and egg transfers allow same-sex partners to conceive biological offspring.

The Heterosexual Assumption

Our culture is built around a subtle but pervasive bias: we are conditioned to live and behave as if everyone were heterosexual. This bias is deeply ingrained in our psyche. Most girls grew up being taught (both explicitly and implicitly) that they would grow into a woman who would marry a man and have babies; boys were taught the same story from the male perspective. Even today there is an enduring assumption that everyone is straight unless revealed to be otherwise, and that it is better to be straight than bisexual, gay, lesbian, transgender, or questioning. This bias can be found in even liberal-minded straight people, including many Unitarian Universalists, who pride themselves in supporting same-sex marriage and fighting for cultural acceptance of same-sex relationships.

This heterosexual bias can be seen in many ways. For example, the media bombard us with images of men and women expressing their attraction and love for each other, while most depictions of homosexual love remain hidden from view. Youth who recognize their sexual identities as gay or lesbian need validation that their interests and attractions are just as acceptable as those of heterosexual youth.

To combat this inherent bias, we must change our assumptions and our mind-set. When we speak to adults, youth, or children, we need to recognize that we may not be aware of their affectional orientation. We need to intentionally communicate to our children and youth that same-sex relationships are valid and have always existed, and that when they grow up, they may be part of a heterosexual relationship or a homosexual relationship, either of which can lead to a lasting commitment.

Gender and Transgender Identity

Adolescents today are given conflicting messages about affectional orientation and gender identity. While there is arguably much more acceptance of BGLTQ persons than there ever was in the past, there is also more violence, harassment, and oppression as their visibility increases. With teenagers coming out at younger ages than ever before, this means straight children, some of whom were raised in bigoted homes, are forced to confront their prejudices and fears at much younger ages, possibly in life stages during which they are less tolerant of differences.

Recent studies reveal that most bisexual, gay, and lesbian youth become aware of their orientation at around ten years old—before many of them have begun puberty, let alone had sexual experiences of any kind. This is encouraging, says Kevin Jennings in *Always My Child*, because it means more young people have a healthy realization of the distinction between sexual identity and sexual behavior. However, because of the pressure BGLTQ youth feel to hide their true identities, most do not come out until several years later— somewhere between ages fifteen and seventeen, on average.

Although some courageous youth are able to live their lives authentically, the majority of our teenagers are still confined to rigid gender roles, and any deviation from those roles brings a harsh penalty. Coaches too often taunt boys for "throwing like a girl" or call them a bunch of sissies or wimps. Boys may be labeled gay (whether they are or not) because they have a preference for singing in the choir or acting in the school play. Although girls are given a bit more flexibility than boys, they too are often forced into rigid stereotypes. A girl who has her heart set on the masculine territory of ice hockey or football, doesn't wear makeup, and prefers sweatpants to skirts is often labeled a "dyke," whether or not she is sexually attracted to other girls.

These conflicting messages about gender conformity can seriously disrupt the major task of adolescence: establishing a sense of identity. Encouraging our children to be open-minded about gender identity becomes even more important as they traverse the difficult waters of middle school, where conformity of all kinds is expected—especially in the area of gender roles. It is during this life stage that boys and girls are increasingly expected to have friends of the same sex and to develop feelings of attraction for the opposite sex. Adolescents who by this time already suspect they may be BGLTQ need emotional strength to break through those rigid ideas of gender that are so prevalent.

Puberty can be a particularly troubling time for transgender youth—those who feel that their inner gender identity is not in sync with their outward biological sex. When they were younger, they may not have felt much pressure to conform to the gender identity that matched their biological sex—a boy may have been allowed to dress and act like a girl or vice versa. But with puberty comes the realization (perhaps for the first time or in a new, tangible way) that they are developing the "wrong" body. When a child who feels like a girl develops facial hair instead of breasts, or a child who feels like a boy begins to menstruate, they can feel repulsed and betrayed by their own body.

Other people may realize that transgender youth are somehow different, but not recognize them for what they truly are. Transgender people are often assumed by others to be lesbian or gay. However, affectional or sexual orientation is distinct and separate from a person's gender identity. Someone who feels like a male and is attracted to other men would be considered gay, but someone who feels like a female (although biologically male) and is attracted to other men is transgender and not gay.

Transgender youth face many of same issues as gay, lesbian, and bisexual adolescents, but also challenges that are unique. The incongruity between their identity and their biology can seem daunting, especially since most of them have no role models for how to be transgender. "These teens may grow up with a deep sense of shame and feel as though they can't express themselves authentically with the body they've been given," writes Jennings. They also face harassment and discrimination even more than do gay, lesbian, and bisexual youth.

Because our culture has such rigid ideas about gender roles and identity, many parents find it hard to accept their child as transgender. Even if your son has seemed feminine from an early age or your daughter is clearly a tomboy, it can still be a shock to learn that your child self-identifies as a different gender. You may unconsciously perceive this as a rejection, particularly if you are of the same biological sex as your child. However, being transgender—like being gay, lesbian, bisexual, or questioning—is not a choice, but a crucial piece of your child's identity.

According to Stephanie Brill and Rachel Pepper in *The Transgendered Child*, some people are coming to recognize that having only two distinct gender categories is extremely limiting. In fact, some believe that if we were to expand the notion of gender identity, many—if not most—people would actually be considered a blend of genders. Many youth and young adults (both BGLTQ and straight) are discovering this notion of a spectrum of gender identity and are pushing for more pronouns than just *he* and *she*. Should this idea ever become prevalent in our society as a whole, life would be much easier for transgender people and others who do not wish to conform to traditional gender roles. Until then, we as parents need to be open to new ideas about gender and encourage our youth to expand their thinking in this regard as well.

Healthy Relationships

Adolescents have intense emotional and sexual feelings and desires. Parents need to respect the intensity of those feelings, even if they seem to be just teenage crushes to us. Although the influence of peer groups increases during adolescence, parents are still the major source of values and judgment. Remain a supportive presence in your teen's life, and make yourself available to answer any questions about relationships and sexuality. Young people who understand their sexuality and are comfortable with it are much more able to develop healthy relationships and cope with their feelings despite peer pressure.

You can also provide guidance to combat the many negative images and stereotypes about sex and relationships in the media. When watching a movie that has a couple engaging in casual sex, comment on how risky it is that they didn't protect themselves. Point out music videos or TV ads that portray women as mere sexual objects, and discuss how most women don't actually look that way.

Talk to your teen about the differences between love and sexual attraction. Explain that love comes in many forms and variations for different people (for instance, love for parents is different than love for a relationship partner), whereas sexual desire involves a strong physical attraction and always carries an element of excitement. From there, it is easier to explain that love can exist without sexual desire, just as sexual desire can exist without love. Communicate that although sometimes two consenting adults might enter into a relationship based on sexual desire alone, sexual relationships are usually healthier when both partners feel love for each other.

Discuss what it means to be part of a couple that is romantically (and perhaps sexually) involved. Emphasize that healthy relationships do not involve power imbalances that serve to coerce either partner into behavior he or she is not ready for.

Many young adults are delaying marriage or committed relationships. While this in itself is not a negative, many of these same young adults, as well as youth, are attempting to meet their sexual needs through casual relationships at great physical risk. Many adolescents are regularly participating in oral-genital stimulation or anal sex because of their perception that this behavior is less risky than engaging in sexual intercourse that could lead to pregnancy. Help your youth understand that all sexual contact that involves the exchange of body fluids carries the risk of sexually transmitted diseases, and that participating in casual sexual activity of any sort can lead to a lifetime of regret.

Letting Go

As Jonas Salk once said, "Good parents give their children roots and wings." Just as roots keep a plant anchored in the ground, the safe, supportive, nurturing environment we give our children helps them feel grounded and secure. And just as a plant extracts nourishment from the soil through its roots, we offer our children nourishment for the soul by articulating our values and beliefs, engaging in spiritual practices with them, and encouraging their faith development.

We also give our children roots through their heritage, which provides a sense of identity and a deep connection to the past. This connection helps them accept themselves and develop the self-confidence they need to strike out on their own. In fact, the very things we do to grow strong roots for our children can also be just what they need to develop their wings of independence— particularly in the area of spiritual and faith development.

As they gain independence, it becomes increasingly clear that our children are complete individuals of their own making. We have all heard of parents who attempt to live vicariously through their children or push them to succeed where they themselves have failed. However, sooner or later we all have to realize that although we can support our children and offer them our guidance, ultimately they must learn to make their own decisions and form their own beliefs.

Since our culture supports an extended adolescence for most young people, the transition to independence is often slow and gradual. But when it does come, it seems in a way that we have been preparing for this very moment from the time our children were born. All parenting is a process of letting go, of accepting that each of our children is his or her own person and a unique individual.

Making Decisions

Since confidence also comes in part from the ability to make decisions, then giving our adolescents the opportunity to make choices and accept the consequences is one way parents give their children the wings they need to fly out of the nest. While our children are young, those choices should be simple and nonthreatening. But by the time they are in high school, adolescents should be able to make some important decisions that involve responsibility and repercussions.

To take healthy risks, adolescents need to trust that the people around them will offer acceptance and support, whatever the outcome. The best way to provide support is not by making decisions for your child, or even suggesting the best option. Rather, it is through offering guidance on *how* to make a decision. Mimi Doe, author of *10 Principles for Spiritual Parenting*, advises that if your child is having trouble making a decision, you can suggest that he ask himself questions like "What is the right thing to do in this situation, according to who I am and what I believe in?" Remind your child to consider what is really important and his own deeply held beliefs.

This opportunity to make mistakes and learn from them is one of the most important opportunities we can give our children while they are still in the security of the home. Likewise, seeing us own up to our own mistakes teaches youth not only that we all have our failings and weaknesses, but that we can choose to own up to our mistakes and do what we can to correct them. When we ask forgiveness for our actions and model forgiveness of others, we strengthen our children's potential to soar.

Instead of being talked down to, youth need to be spoken to as equals. Show respect for their decisions, even if they are not the ones you would have made or wish they had made. Recognize that at some point you can no longer make all the important decisions for them, but can only encourage them to make the best possible decisions.

Fitting In or Standing Out

Among adolescents, any appearance of being different can result in rejection. This can be daunting for youth as they try to develop a positive self-identity and find a place in the social structure of their peers. Instead of receiving positive affirmation in the spirit of "I'm okay, you're okay," teens who don't fit in are too often teased or ostracized. Since adolescents remain egocentric, their fear of rejection can border on obsession. A teen may be mortified at the thought that everyone will notice the sweat stains on her gym clothes or the pimple that just sprouted on his forehead.

Some creative youth will turn this fear of rejection around and deliberately create an appearance which draws attention or amplifies their uniqueness. Since they often feel as if they are the center of attention, embracing this can mean sporting unusual hair styles (and color), clothing, or make-up. In recent years, tattoos and multiple body piercings also have become ways adolescents take ownership of their uniqueness. Instead of dwelling upon any rejection which results from non-conformity, they consider their bodies as an artist's palette to be adorned and decorated with the intent to attract the most attention possible. Because there is pain involved in both piercings and obtaining tattoos, their visibility speaks to other youth who have also adopted such adornments and serves to bond them together in a shared experience. In fact, piercings and tattoos can be viewed as a kind of rite of passage that youth bestow upon themselves.

Choosing a Religious Path

Our teens' independence of thought and decision-making is perhaps most difficult to accept in the area of spirituality. So often parents feel as though they have failed when their adult children choose a different religious path. In particular, parents who have rejected the religious teachings of their childhood may be dismayed to find that their teen or young adult children are reclaiming those very same religious traditions. This is what theologian Harvey Cox refers to as the "third generation phenomenon," when children embrace the religion of their grandparents rather than that of their parents. It can be hard for parents to not take this personally.

Although we can communicate our beliefs and share our spiritual practices with our children, we need to recognize that they will eventually choose their own path and that their journey may take them in a very different direction. Their decision is not necessarily a rejection of us and our ideas, but their own way of discovering meaning in life. Remember, too, that even if your children do not adopt your spiritual practices as their own, they might still view them as beloved traditions that evoke special memories because of the value that you place on them. As Jeanne Nieuwejaar explains in *The Gift of Faith*, "We cannot choose whether [our children] will be religious, but we can choose how and to what extent we will support, guide, and celebrate this dimension of their nature."

A New Relationship

Sooner or later, there comes a time when all parents must acknowledge that their active involvement in their children's lives has come to a close. This usually occurs when a child takes charge of his own life. Yet, as Elizabeth Berger describes in *Raising Kids With Character*, "There is in all bonds between parents and children an ebb and flow, and a depth of attachment such that even into adulthood, middle age, and in some cases, old age, the tie between them continues to be deepened by new shared experiences."

While the days of active parenting may be over, we remain parents until the day we or our children are no longer part of this world. The relationship may change, but we will always hold a special place in their lives, just as they will never cease to be our children. Our legacy is the love we offer them and the foundation we give them on which to build their own values. And our immortality lies in the values, beliefs, and ideals they received from us and will pass on to their own children.

We start our children on their journey and travel with them for as long as we are able to do so. But in a real sense, parenting is a long process of letting go. From the toddler who pulls away and insists "Me do!" to the adolescent who struggles to separate his identity from that of his parents, our children experience an ever-increasing series of separations from us. When their wings are ready, we can only watch them go and hope that we gave them the roots to find their own way in the world.

For Further Reading

For Adults

Bartlett, Jane. *Parenting with Spirit: 30 Ways to Nurture Your Child's Spirit and Enrich Your Family's Life*. New York: Marlowe & Co., 2004.

Berger, Elizabeth. *Raising Kids with Character: Developing Trust and Integrity in Children*. Lanham, MD: Rowman and Littlefield, 2004.

Bernstein, Robert. *Straight Parents, Gay Children: Inspiring Families to Live Honestly and with Greater Understanding*. New York: Thunder's Mouth Press, 1999.

Brill, Stephanie, and Rachel Pepper. *The Transgendered Child: A Handbook for Families and Professionals*. San Francisco: Cleis Publishing, 2008.

Butash, Adrian. *Bless This Food: Ancient and Contemporary Graces From Around the World*. Novato, CA: New World Library, 2007.

Coles, Robert. *The Moral Life of Children*. Boston, MA: Atlantic Monthly Press, 1986.

———. *The Spiritual Life of Children*. Boston, MA: Houghton Mifflin, 1990.

Cornell, Joseph Bharat. *Sharing Nature with Children: A Parents' and Teachers' Nature-Awareness Guidebook*. Nevada City, CA: Ananda Publications, 1979.

Cox, Meg. *The Book of New Family Traditions: How to Create Great Rituals for Holidays and Everyday.* Philadelphia: Running Press, 2003.

Desmond, Lisa. *Baby Buddhas: A Guide for Teaching Meditation to Children.* Kansas City, MO: Andrews McMeel Publishing, 2004.

Doe, Mimi, and Marsha Walch. *10 Principles for Spiritual Parenting: Nurturing Your Child's Soul.* New York: HarperPerennial, 1998.

Doe, Mimi. *Nurturing Your Teenager's Soul: A Practical Approach to Raising a Kind, Honorable, Compassionate Teen.* New York: Penguin Books, 2004.

Dougy Center. *35 Ways to Help a Grieving Child.* Portland, OR: Dougy Center, 1999.

Fuchs, Nancy. *Our Share of Night, Our Share of Morning: Parenting as a Spiritual Journey.* San Francisco: HarperSanFrancisco, 1996.

Gellman, Marc and Thomas Hartman. *Where Does God Live? Questions and Answers for Parents and Children.* New York: Triumph Books, 1991.

Grille, Robin. *Parenting for a Peaceful World.* Richmond, VA: Children's Project, 2008.

Haffner, Debra. *From Diapers to Dating: A Parent's Guide to Raising Sexually Healthy Children.* New York: Newmarket Press, 2004.

Hoertdoerfer, Patricia, ed. *The Parent Guide to Our Whole Lives: Grades K–1 and Grades 4–6.* Boston: Unitarian Universalist Association, 2000.

Isay, Jane. *Walking on Eggshells: Navigating the Delicate Relationship Between Adult Children and Parents.* New York: Doubleday/Flying Dolphin Press, 2007.

Jennings, Kevin. *Always My Child: A Parent's Guide to Understanding Your Gay, Lesbian, Bisexual, Transgendered or Questioning Son or Daughter.* New York: Simon & Schuster, 2003.

Kabat-Zinn, Myla, and Jon Kabat-Zinn. *Everyday Blessings: The Inner Work of Mindful Parenting.* New York: Hyperion, 1997.

Kushner, Harold. *When Children Ask About God: A Guide for Parents Who Don't Always Have All the Answers.* New York: Schoken Books, 1989.

Lang, Virginia, and Louise Nayer. *How to Bury a Goldfish and Other Ceremonies and Celebrations for Everyday Life.* Boston: Skinner House, 2007.

Levine, Madeline. *The Price of Privilege: How Parental Pressure and Material Advantage Are Creating a Generation of Disconnected and Unhappy Kids.* New York: HarperCollins, 2006.

Madden, Kristin. *Pagan Parenting: Spiritual, Magical and Emotional Development of the Child.* Niceville, FL: Spilled Candy Publications, 2004.

McCarty, Marietta. *Little Big Minds: Sharing Philosophy with Kids.* New York: Penguin, 2006.

McGowan, Dale, ed. *Parenting Beyond Belief: On Raising Ethical, Caring Kids Without Religion.* New York: American Management Association, 2007.

McGowan, Dale, Molleen Matsumura, Amanda Metzkas, and Jan Devor. *Raising Freethinkers: A Practical Guide for Parenting Beyond Belief.* New York: AMACOM, 2009.

Nieuwejaar, Jeanne Harrison. *The Gift of Faith: Tending the Spiritual Lives of Children.* Boston: Skinner House Books, 2003.

Pickett, Helen. *Rejoice Together: Prayers, Meditations, and Other Readings for Family, Individual and Small Group Worship.* Boston: Skinner House, 1995.

Pipher, Mary. *Reviving Ophelia: Saving the Selves of Adolescent Girls.* New York: Putnam, 1994.

————. *The Shelter of Each Other: Rebuilding Our Families.* New York: G.P. Putnam & Sons, 1996.

Prothero, Stephen. *Religious Literacy: What Every American Needs to Know and Doesn't.* San Francisco, CA: HarperSanFracisco, 2007.

Roberts, Elizabeth, and Elias Amidon. *Earth Prayers: 365 Prayers, Poems, and Invocations for Honoring the Earth.* San Francisco: Harper-SanFrancisco, 1991.

————. *Life Prayers: 365 Prayers, Blessings, and Affirmations to Celebrate the Human Journey.* San Francisco: HarperSanFrancisco, 1996.

Robinson, Jo, and Jean Coppock Staeheli. *Unplug the Christmas Machine: A Complete Guide to Putting Love and Joy Back into the Season.* New York: Quill, 1991.

Ryan, M.J. *A Grateful Heart: Daily Blessings for the Evening Meal from Buddha to the Beatles.* San Francisco: Conari Press, 1994.

For Children

Adoff, Arnold. *Black Is Brown Is Tan.* New York: HarperCollins Publishers, 2002.

Baylor, Byrd. *Everybody Needs a Rock.* New York: Scribner, 1985.

Bennett, Helen. *Humanism—What's That? A Book for Curious Kids.* Amherst, NY: Prometheus Books, 2005.

Blanchard, Eliza. *A Child's Book of Blessings and Prayers.* Boston: Skinner House, 2008.

Boritzer, Etan. *What is Death?* Venice, CA: Veronica Lane Books, 2000.

————. *What is God?* Tonawanda, NY: Firefly Books, 1990.

————. *What is Right?* Venice, CA: Veronica Lane Books, 2005.

Boroson, Martin. *Becoming Me: A Story of Creation*. Woodstock, VT: Skylight Paths Pub., 2000.

Brotman, Charlene. *The Kids' Book of Awesome Stuff*. Biddeford, ME: Brotman Marshfield, 2004.

Brown, Laurie Krasny. *When Dinosaurs Die: A Guide to Understanding Death*. Boston, MA: Little, Brown, 1996.

Brown, Laurie Krasny, and Marc Brown. *What's the Big Secret? Talking about Sex with Girls and Boys*. Boston, MA: Little, Brown & Co., 1997.

Carbone, Christopher Kavi. *Namaste! Songs, Yoga and Meditations for Young Yogis*. Newport, RI: Arts in Celebration, 2005. Audio CD.

Conrad, Heather. *Lights of Winter: Winter Celebrations Around the World*. Berkeley, CA: Lightport Books, 2001.

Couper, Heather, with Nigel Henbest. *Big Bang—The Story of the Universe*. New York: DK Publishing, 1997.

Curtis, Chara M. *All I See Is Part of Me*. Bellevue, WA: Illumination Arts Pub. Co., 1994.

Davol, Marguerite W. *Black, White, Just Right!* Morton Grove, IL: Albert Whitman, 1993.

Demi. *The Empty Pot*. St. Paul, MN: Minnesota Humanities Commission, Motheread/Fatheread-MN, 2000.

Dillon, Leo, and Diane Dillon. *To Everything There Is a Season*. New York: Harcourt Brace Jovanovich, 1979.

Edwards, Carolyn McVickar. *The Return of the Light: Twelve Tales from Around the World for the Winter Solstice*. New York: Marlowe, 2000.

Garland, Sherry. *The Lotus Seed*. San Diego, CA: Harcourt Brace Jovanovich, 1993.

Garth, Maureen. *Earthlight: New Meditations for Children*. Dublin: Gil and MacMillan, 1998.

———. *Moonbeam: A Book of Meditations for Children*. Perth, WA: CollinsDove, 1992.

———. *Starbright: Meditations for Children*. San Francisco: Harper-SanFrancisco, 1991.

———. *Sunshine: More Meditations for Children*. Perth, WA: Collins-Dove, 1994.

Gellman, Mark. *Does God Have a Big Toe? Stories About Stories in the Bible*. New York: Harper & Row, 1989.

Gordon, Sol. *All Families Are Different*. Amherst, NY: Prometheus, 2000.

Gunney, Lynn Tuttle. *Meet Jesus: The Life and Lessons of a Beloved Teacher*. Boston: Skinner House Books, 2007.

Harris, Robie H., and Michael Emberley. *It's Not the Stork! A Book about Girls, Boys, Babies, Bodies, Families, and Friends*. Cambridge, MA: Candlewick, 2006.

———. *It's Perfectly Normal: Changing Bodies, Growing Up, Sex, and Sexual Health*. Cambridge, MA: Candlewick, 1994.

———. *It's So Amazing! A Book about Eggs, Sperm, Birth, Babies, and Families*. Cambridge, MA: Candlewick: 1999.

Jackson, Ellen. *Earth Mother*. New York: Walker & Co., 2005.

———. *The Winter Solstice*. Brookfield, CT: Millbook Press, 1994.

Katz, Karen. *The Colors of Us*. New York: Henry Holt and Co., 1999.

Kissinger, Katie. *All the Colors We Are: The Story of How We Get Our Skin Color*. St. Paul, MN: Redleaf Press, 1994.

Kowalski, Gary. *Earth Day: An Alphabet Book*. Boston: Skinner House, 2009.

Kushner, Lawrence, and Karen Kushner. *Because Nothing Looks Like God*. Woodstock, VT: Jewish Lights Publishing, 2000.

Lewis, Barbara. *The Kids' Guide to Service Projects: Over 500 Service Ideas for Young People Who Want to Make a Difference.* Minneapolis, MN: Free Spirit Publishing, 1995.

————. *The Kids' Guide to Social Action: How to Solve the Social Problems You Choose—And Turn Creative Thinking into Positive Action.* Minneapolis, MN: Free Spirit Publishing, 1991.

Martignacco, Carole. *The Everything Seed: A Story of Beginnings.* Berkeley, CA: Tricycle Press, 2006.

Matthews, Caitlin. *The Blessing Seed: A Creation Myth for a New Millennium.* Cambridge, MA: Barefoot Books, 2000.

McCloud, Carol. *Have You Filled a Bucket Today? A Guide to Daily Happiness for Kids.* Northville, MI: Ferne Press, 2006.

McCutcheon, Marc. *The Beast in You! Activities and Questions to Explore Evolution.* Charlotte, VT: Williamson Publishing, 1999.

McNulty, Faith. *How Whales Walked into the Sea.* New York: Scholastic Press, 1999.

Mellonie, Bryan. *Lifetimes: A Beautiful Way to Explain Death to Children.* New York: Bantam, 1983.

Moore, Mary Ann. *Hide and Seek with God.* Boston: Skinner House Books, 1994.

Morgan, Jennifer. *Born with a Bang: The Universe Tells Its Cosmic Story, Book One.* Nevada City, CA: Dawn Publications, 2002.

————. *From Lava to Life: The Universe Tells Its Cosmic Story, Book Two.* Nevada City, CA: Dawn Publications, 2003.

————. *Mammals Who Morph: The Universe Tells Its Cosmic Story, Book Three.* Nevada City, CA: Dawn Publications, 2006.

Muth, John. *Zen Shorts.* New York: Scholastic, 2005.

————. *The Shortest Day: Celebrating the Winter Solstice.* New York: Dutton Children's Books, 2003.

Rice, David. *Because Brian Hugged His Mother.* Nevada City, CA: Dawn Publications, 1999.

Richardson, Justin and Parnell, Peter. *And Tango Makes Three.* New York: Simon & Schuster, 2005

Romain, Trevor. *What on Earth Do You Do When Someone Dies?* Minneapolis, MN: Free Spirit Publishing, 1999.

Sasso, Sandy Eisenberg. *Butterflies Under Our Hats.* Brewster, MA: Paraclete Press, 2006.

————. *God in Between.* Woodstock, VT: Jewish Lights, 1998.

————. *God's Paintbrush.* Woodstock, VT: Jewish Lights, 1992.

Viorst, Judith. *The Tenth Good Thing About Barney.* New York: Aladdin Paperbacks, 1987.

White Deer of Autumn. *The Great Change.* Hillsboro, OR: Beyond Words Publishing, 1992.

Wood, Douglas. *Grandad's Prayers of the Earth.* Cambridge, MA: Candlewick, 1999.

————. *Old Turtle.* New York, NY: Scholastic Press, 1992

————. *Old Turtle and the Broken Truth.* New York: Scholastic Press, 2003.

Zolotow, Charlotte. *The Hating Book.* New York: Harper & Row, 1969.

For Youth

Bell, Ruth. *Changing Bodies, Changing Lives.* New York: Times Books, 1998.

Canfield, Jack, Mark Victor Hanson, Kimberly Kirberger, and Mitch Claspy. *Chicken Soup for the Teenage Soul: 101 Stories of Life, Love and Learning.* Deerfield Beach, FL: Health Communications, 1997.

Chopra, Deepak. *Fire in the Heart: A Spiritual Guide for Teens.* New York: Simon and Schuster Books for Young Readers, 2004.

Fitzgerald, Helen. *The Grieving Teen: A Guide for Teenagers and Their Friends.* New York: Simon & Schuster, 2000.

Gootman, Marilyn, and Pamela Espeland. *When a Friend Dies: A Book for Teens About Grieving and Healing.* Minneapolis: Free Spirit Publishing, 2005.

Halpin, Mikki. *It's Your World—If You Don't Like It, Change It: Activism for Teenagers.* New York: Simon Pulse, 2004.

Huegel, Kelly. *GLBTQ: The Survival Guide for Queer and Questioning Teens.* Minneapolis, MN: Free Spirit Publishing, 2003.

Keen, Lisa. *Out Law: What LGBT Youth Should Know.* Boston: Beacon Press, 2007.

Lewis, Barbara. *The Teen Guide to Global Action: How to Connect with Others to Create Social Change.* Minneapolis: Free Spirit Publications, 2008.

————. *What Do You Stand For? A Teen's Guide to Building Character.* Minneapolis: Freespirit, 2005.

Lite, Lori. *Indigo Teen Dreams: Guided Meditation-Relaxation Techniques Designed to Decrease Stress, Anger and Anxiety While Increasing Self-Esteem and Self-Awareness.* Marietta, GA: Litebooks.net, 2004. Audio CD.

Loundin, Sumi. *Blue Jean Buddha: Voices of Young Buddhists.* Boston, MA: Wisdom Publications, 2001.

Metcalf, Franz. *Buddha in Your Backpack: Everyday Buddhism for Teens.* Berkeley, CA: Seastone/Ulysses Press, 2002.

Owens, Robert. *Queer Kids: The Challenges and Promise for Lesbian, Gay, and Bisexual Youth.* New York: Haworth Press, 1998.

Acknowledgments

Special thanks go to my husband, Bryan, and my two children for their patience and willingness to give up computer time so I could edit and revise; to all of the religious educators who forwarded my parent survey to families in their congregation, but especially Rev. Colleen McDonald, Roy Sumner, and Terry Ward; to Andrea Lerner, Betty Jo Middleton, Layne Richard Hammock, and Linda Volkersz for their suggestions on UU holidays; and to Mindy Whisenhunt, Annette Long, Patty French, Catie Chi, Cara Cook, Janet French, and Ruth Gibson for sharing their personal stories.

I am indebted to all of the parents who submitted surveys or sent emails with their responses about Unitarian Universalist parenting: Lisa Apostolopoulos-Powell, Ellen Bordman, David Bright, Anne Bristol, Darwin Bromley, Robin Brzozowski, Christina Caglar, Kathleen Carpenter, Melanie Constantinides, Roy Ellzey, Rachel Gerberding, Jennifer Glassmann, Christine Gresser, Liz Grimes, Lynn Gunney, Robert Hamm, LeAnn Hanna, Jody Horn, Louise Klatt, Linda Lawrence, Jeff Liebmann, Dave Moffat, Leo Nagorski, Lisa Noble, Anne Odom, Teresa Okann, Peggy Olsen-Missildine, Jen Pots, Nancy Patterson, Christine Prado, Kelly Riney, Jeanett Ruyle, Mary Beth Schillinger, Christine Sizer, Liz Steere, Rita Storey, Donna Stram, Sharron Mendel Swain, Teresa Wilmot, David Wright, Laura Yamashita, Korin Zigler, and countless other Unitarian Universalist parents who shared their stories but wish to remain anonymous.

I would also like to thank some of the many Unitarian Universalist parents whom I know personally and who have inspired me through their parenting, which I have witnessed firsthand: Krista Bailey and Greg Koehler, Chris and Patty French, Annette Long and Terry Mark, Amy and Kevin DeBeck, Laura Snow and Dan Watson, Gail and Allen deSomer, Tama Crisovan and Rich Wallace, Jenny Singer and John Dolezal, Liz Rinehart, and Tom Barry.

Last but not least, I would like to thank all of my "favorite" Unitarian Universalist youth and young adults: Rochelle Liechty, A.J. Phillips, Eric Weigold, Megan Weigold, Sara Weigold, Heather Weigold, Justin Dolezal, Allison Dolezal, Anna Dolezal, Laura Dolezal, Laurel Cherniak, Rebecca Fisette, Lizzie French, Elise deSomer, Kyra Treibold, and of course, my own adolescent daughter, Shannon Richards.